THE STALLED SOCIETY

ALSO BY MICHEL CROZIER
The Bureaucratic Phenomenon
The World of the Office Worker

MICHEL CROZIER

THE STALLED SOCIETY

THE VIKING PRESS ● NEW YORK

La Société Bloquée

© Éditions du seuil, 1970

English language translation Copyright © 1973
by The Viking Press, Inc.

First published in 1973 by The Viking Press, Inc.
625 Madison Avenue, New York, N.Y. 10022

Published simultaneously in Canada by
The Macmillan Company of Canada Limited

SBN 670-66687-4

Library of Congress catalog card number: 73-9066

Printed in U.S.A. by The Colonial Press Inc.

The stalled society with which this work is primarily concerned is French society. Although France is a changing society, it is severely restricted by its straitjacket of centralized administration, its caste system impervious to any form of communication, and its rigid style of education and models of thinking that are completely hostile to any form of experiment. The more French society changes, the more acute its problems of collective organization become, and the more it suffocates. We should not assume that the French are unwilling to change. On the contrary, they are feverishly active in this regard. But their ideologies are compensating, not motive, forces, and their violent criticisms and recriminations, which they express in very concrete terms, merely serve to strengthen their traditional modes of administration, communication, and reasoning.

French society is not the only stalled society. Blockages seem to be an essential characteristic of modern advanced societies. Because of the increasing pace of change, because of the increasing interdependence of individuals and of groups, because the social tissue of each country is becoming more and more complex and vulnerable, these societies are forced to look for new forms of government and administration. A slow, obscure process of social experimentation is taking place, but this alone cannot change the main forms of social regulation and the models of action essential to any collective undertaking. Meanwhile, we can observe, in society as a whole and in all those interacting human systems composing it, a multitude of blockages that lend their tone to the overall system. Even in day-to-day transactions, people are trapped in vicious circles; whatever their intentions, the logic of the system distorts their activities and forces them to collaborate in preserving the model. We cannot trust evolution to solve this problem.

Instead, our age would seem to be characterized by involution—as if our human resources, our models of intervention, change, and progress, were crystallizing and becoming rigid. At the same time, we are becoming aware of their inadequacy and ineffectiveness—as if our entire culture, our stock of experience and reasoning, were a burden rather than a source of strength.

This work, which is no more than an essay, cannot hope to provide an answer to this immense problem, for it is one which, in my opinion, goes deeper than questions of political ideology or values. What I have tried to do is throw some light on the question by analyzing the difficulties facing French society. I have not attempted to approach the subject in terms of the peculiarities of French society seen in comparison with the norms of Western society as a whole—which has often been done. On the contrary, I have tried to see French society as an example that will help us better understand the mechanisms governing the blockages and the processes of involution now paralyzing all advanced societies.

The relevance of the French example to British and American society may be disputed. The differences are obvious, of course, and, on the face of it, it is much easier to draw up a traveler's notebook or a classical anthropologist's inventory, attributing a character to this or that set of customs and then trying to define its essence. But the new uses of comparative analysis go well beyond this kind of exotic interest in other societies. What interests us today is no longer our neighbor's unique "essence," but the very special sum of successes and failures he has accumulated as a result of his particular essence. What interests us is the laboratory experiment our neighbor represents for us, because his very foreignness allows us to analyze in a clearer context mechanisms that are much harder to understand in our own country.

The first part of this book is devoted to problems concerning human relationships and collective management, to systems where blockages occur, and to the effect of knowledge on them. These chapters were written on the basis of sociological research carried out in France, but they are centered on what I consider to be a fundamental universal phenomenon, one which now constitutes the last taboo in the Western world—the phenomenon of power. This has been dealt with no better in Great Britain and the United States than in France.

In Part II, this discussion and analysis are applied to French society. The basic questions we have to answer are: Why does French society allow itself to be constrained by its bureaucratic, paternalistic straitjacket? Why do the French spend their time reinforcing the system from which they suffer, even when they revile it? And how can they change? How could they change, and how could knowledge help them change in better ways? It is impossible to answer these questions directly, but we can answer them by analyzing how the main blockage mechanisms function in their two most opposed manifestations: the impersonal, hierarchic order—the bureaucratic vicious circle dominating the country's government, public life, official institutions; and the disorder and revolutionary ferment which has always been endemic but which once again revealed itself in full in the crisis of May 1968.

Part III is devoted to a discussion of action, and of the directions change is likely to take in modern societies. I discuss here both general problems of intellectual method and sociological methodology, and possible applications for French society.

This book was born out of long experience in sociological research in France, out of numerous dialogues while teaching at Harvard University between 1967 and 1970, and out of ten years of civic action as a member of the Club Jean Moulin in

Paris. My final choices are personal ones, but they are the fruit of this ceaseless dialogue, which has enabled me to look beyond the narrow horizons of the French university researcher.

I dedicate this book to my associates and friends at the Centre de Sociologie des Organisations; to my students, colleagues, and friends at Harvard, especially Stanley Hoffmann; and to my old comrades at the Club Jean Moulin. It is as much the outcome of their reactions as of my propositions.

Michel Crozier
August 8, 1972

CONTENTS

THE STALLED SOCIETY

INTRODUCTION

The Responsibilities of the Sociologist

I express myself as a sociologist, and it is as such that I take sides on the issues facing modern society. That is to say, my contribution has been shaped by a certain type of knowledge, one which depends on analytical methods, on certain modes of reasoning, and therefore on a specific logic.

This logic is misunderstood, despite the increasingly widespread diffusion of the social sciences. Mistakenly, the social scientist is the object both of groundless fears and of ill-considered enthusiasm. The reader should know the true nature of the social-science contribution, for it is very partial but also very specific. The social scientist does bear some responsibility in our crisis-ridden society. But we must assess his responsibility in the light of his actual comprehension, not in terms of society's needs and dreams.

Reality and Fiction in the Social Sciences

In recent years, whenever a journalist or essayist has wanted to discuss the "human density" of a situation, he has found himself invoking the agents—the "context," the "background"—of "sociological forces." This sloppy use of the epithet "sociological" misleads the public badly by giving it the wholly wrong

3

impression that the social sciences are widely practiced and that their practice is both arbitrary and dangerous. The man who explains something as being due to the "sociological context" is not offering an explanation capable of being contested, researched, or verified; he is suggesting an extraordinary spiderweb of strictly determinist factors, an image destroying our last illusions of freedom.

Nothing could be more false. The few genuine researchers, teachers, and practitioners who use techniques or methods inspired by sociology or social psychology have not the slightest influence on the conduct of affairs. The influence of the social sciences in Europe, especially in France and Italy, in the education of the younger generation is laughably small when compared with that of literature and philosophy. The recent taste for sociology among students in the humanities has not helped at all to spread the findings of scientific sociology, and the explosion of May 1968 temporarily compromised the cautious progress we had made.

Some may still say that sociology is potentially dangerous. By stripping and dismantling the mainsprings of human behavior in society, sociology and social psychology make it easier to manipulate and control people. If we allow this to continue, it will no longer be possible to be a revolutionary or even an innovator without being considered a deviant, possibly even being treated as one. People are afraid that the social scientist will demonstrate that social conflicts are absurd, and thus deprive society of the yeast of activity, progress, and innovation.

But this is a childish argument. If the conflicts are real, the slightest intellectual rigor will oblige us to recognize their true dimensions, and if they are not real, then the sociologist's work will help us discover the true conflicts hidden behind the false oppositions. The scientific nature of the sociologist's work, far from suppressing conflict, makes it emerge with greater clarity; in other words, conflict becomes more concrete—and more human.

A number of sociologists (though few in France) have deluded themselves that concord and harmony are "better" than struggle and conflict, and that their knowledge could be put to the service of their humanist enthusiasms. But in all scientific disciplines generous souls have harbored such illusions without seriously damaging the progress of their science, and we may note that a large number of more or less Fourierist radicals share this illusion that it is possible to build a harmonious, conflict-free society.

In more conservative circles, it is often held that sociology, in essence determinist, is a threat to man's freedom. When the day comes that the human factor can be introduced into a machine, there will be nothing left for man to decide, since the solution that will ensure the greatest happiness of the greatest number will be discoverable scientifically. This coarse vision is as naïve today for the human sciences as it was a century ago for the physical sciences. Any real progress in knowledge, any movement toward a more complex level of explanation, far from locking us into a web of rigid determinisms, makes us aware of a new series of problems and new forms of freedom we were incapable of imagining before.

In some administrative and managerial circles, finally, it is blandly declared that sociologists devote huge amounts of effort (and money) only to demonstrate what everyone already knew. There may sometimes be, unfortunately, more truth in this argument than in the one put forward by the radicals. But no scientific discipline is exempt from these risks, and, in view of the actual amounts of money available to sociologists, the wastage is certainly far less than in the physical sciences.

Perhaps the hardest thing for sociologists to cope with is the apparently commonsensical nature of the problems they deal with, since everyone thinks he has all the information he needs on the subject in order to explain away all the apparent contradictions. But in reality, what one calls an evident truth is just a commonly accepted proposition, one which is contradicted by two or three other propositions that are just as commonly accepted. On a few occasions in the course of surveys that I and my colleagues conducted among French businesses, we made bets with some executives and managers as to which "evident truths" would emerge from our work. We had not the heart to remind them of their predictions when the results emerged. Determining which is the correct one among various possible opinions may not at first sight appear to be a worthy subject for creative work; but one can see that from the point of view of the advancement of knowledge it at least lets us make a little progress.

The sociologist's creative work lies both elsewhere and beyond this. It consists in elaborating potentially fruitful hypotheses—testing them, interpreting the results, and, on the basis of more advanced knowledge, proposing new original ideas that will stimulate further thinking. It is a modest business, as any truly scientific venture is, but it enables us slowly to nibble away at the unknown. It is on this kind of work that the sociologist would like to be judged.

He desires neither to frighten nor to beguile. He knows he cannot provide answers to those enormous questions we would like him to answer (and at the same time have fears that he might find the answers after all). But he knows that he can make a serious contribution to the advancement of knowledge—more precisely, to man's understanding of the conditions and consequences of his actions—and that his efforts will eventually be more important in the building of the future than even the most seductive speculations.

The Acceleration of Change and the Transformation of Sociology

The reader will not find in these opening words—in this virtual profession of faith—the popularly accepted caricature of the sociologist as he has been known since the heyday of student revolt in the late 1960s. The social sciences in general, and sociology in particular, invariably played a central role in the ferment then. And while the conventional image of the "committed sociologist" gives a somewhat misleading idea of reality, it is not completely false. Most social scientists were deeply shaken by the revolutionary explosion of 1968, and many were directly involved. Since then, sociology has undergone a more profound crisis than any other discipline or intellectual profession. The "realistic" behavior model I outlined above exists, perhaps is even more vigorous than before, but its practitioners are still in the minority—as compared to the more or less "committed" types of sociologists. These latter bear witness, more than to any capacity for scientific analysis, to the uncertainties of our times.

Yet the current confusion and sense of crisis well illustrate the very serious issues now emerging as a result of a transformation in conditions and methods of action, in a world where the pace of change is rapidly accelerating. Although the social sciences have so far played no part in this, the issues are becoming crucial, inasmuch as they appear to stem from man's growing anguish when faced with the new responsibilities imposed on him by this transformation. So the crisis of sociology as well as its popularity have not occurred by mere chance, even if they have nothing to do with present-day realities. They are the result of a sudden awareness, among the elite of Western youth, of this radical transformation in the traditional relations between action and the social sciences.

Why is this so?

It is worth reflecting a little longer on this problem, since by examining it we should be able to evaluate more precisely the intellectual's role and responsibility in the contemporary world. Until now, the sociologist has lived as an ideologist, sheltered from the harsh reality of conflicts that disturb societies. Not that he lacked passion, prejudice, and bias; not that he had no intellectual influence. But his influence was seen in matters of theory and principle, not where responsible decision-making was concerned. His analytical methods directed him toward either descriptive or normative research. Of course, description could develop into revelation and demystification, thus shaking the foundations of the established order, and prescriptive research could turn into commitment and combativity. But science *qua* science remained the lofty kingdom of ideas.

In a society where change occurred slowly, hypotheses about the functioning of institutions could be constructed free from conscious and responsible reflection about possible human intervention. The use of more objective methods enabled man to perceive the illusions of leaders blinded by superficial power, while the technological revolution transformed the structures on which those leaders depended. By more or less skillfully extrapolating from analysis of the past to anticipation of the future, from knowledge of contradiction to its resolution, philosophers and sociologists were content to speculate on how societies evolved or on what sort of revolution would force them to begin all over again (perhaps for the last time). Either way, they believed that both partial evolution and liberating revolution were beyond the powers of man's deliberate and rational will. Revolutionary war, charged as it was with chiliastic emotion, was not very different, after all, from the wars of religion.

The frustrations arising out of this dichotomy between a narrowly positivist world of thought and a world of action still dominated by moral and religious principles paved the way for the success of Marxism. Science and morality at the same time, Marxism effectively squared the circle whereby man could be made whole again. This was possible only by reducing scientific description to the level of rigid functionalism, and stripping moral commitment of all existential depth. It was a heavy price to pay, but the thirst for wholeness and coherence was so great that thought of this was driven out of men's minds.

We are now in a position to re-examine these forms of reasoning. The speeding up of change has wholly transformed our understanding of our responsibilities. We now live long enough to witness the consequences of our actions. Society is forced to become conscious of the choices it makes. Of course, for a long time to come the complexity of the variables involved will obscure knowledge. But if we are taking a long time to tear away the veil, it is more because we are unwilling than because we are incapable. Despite resistance, the social sciences are already making experimental advances where individuals and small groups are concerned, and it is now possible to set up exploratory experiments regarding complex organizations or institutions.

This change in perspective will, in the long run, be as important as the Galilean revolution. It dooms all ideologies, even if paradoxically it rehabilitates a utopian vision we had come to look upon as outmoded. The methodology of decision-making currently being developed tends to suppress the traditional dichotomy between ends and means. Once it succeeds in substituting experimental social sciences for the dogmatic or merely descriptive disciplines of the past, we cannot but advance, in the field of social organization also, from a form of reasoning based on the priority of principles to one based on the priority of experiment.

This has not yet developed very far. But its potentialities, which are already clear, are so disturbing to our traditional concept of the world that it is easy to understand how they have come to provoke a violent backlash. As in every great cultural mutation of the past, the crisis we are observing today reveals a very powerful revolutionary ferment. Perhaps we shall be able to avoid the major upheavals that have disturbed Western society in the past—at the time of the Reformation, for example—but the intellectual problems facing us today are of the same magnitude.

It is hardly surprising, in the face of such far-reaching cultural change, that the reactions of those engaged in intellectual adventure should be so deeply contradictory. Some thinkers have tended to overestimate the immediate possibilities of comprehension and intervention, and to inflate the possible degree of rationality to the point of dreaming of total mastery over all human determinisms. Others have rushed, panic-stricken, back to first sources and principles, carried on a great wave of "fundamentalist" fanaticism denying both science and reason.

These two impulses clash and converge, not only within the same society and within the same circles, but even within the same individuals. The rationalist arrogance that has long been characteristic of American liberal thought is not, for example, completely absent from the current anarchist trend. Many of today's anarchists delude themselves, when necessary, into believing that once we have attained total transparency in our human relations, the rational capacities of computers will suffice to keep society on an even keel.

Perhaps the disproportion is surprising between the highly intellectual nature of the problems raised and the emotional force of the reactions we can observe everywhere around us. But these problems, like the ones dramatized by Luther, call into question some of the most sacred elements of our world view.

After all, that society should come to know the forces governing it, and that it should consequently exercise control over itself, is a rather terrifying prospect. Our former stability was created on a basis of ignorance and impotence. Now a better understanding of reality and of our own potential is forcing us to act. But in the name of what are we to act? How can we act in the name of a higher authority, when traditional goals are being discredited? And yet, how can we refuse to act, when we are daily confronted with scandals that are clearly the consequences of human actions?

The movement of idol-smashing fury experienced by the Western world during the 1960s (a movement that is still with us) developed out of these painful contradictions. It is they which provoked this extraordinary throwback to irrational, temporarily uncontrollable affectivity, more reminiscent of an Islamic holy war than like an intellectual movement.

One way to avoid the agony of choosing would be to smash the mirror. It would be easy to show that it was a distorting mirror—but the reason we instinctively reproach it is not because it distorts, but because it reveals too much. The fanatical reaffirmation of primitive Marxist principles at their most threadbare—most thoroughly refuted by experience— bears witness to this. *Credo quia absurdum:* people want to reassure themselves by appealing to faith—that is, by returning to that state of innocence now threatened by the treacherous fruit of knowledge.

Sociologists and the Problems Caused by Change

Confronted with these facile illusions and in the face of this precipitate regression, are sociologists really equipped to deal effectively with the problems of change?

The answer must be definitely not, if they continue to pontificate and be dogmatic, if they continue in attitudes inherited from their ideological past. But yes, perhaps, if they can bring themselves to accept the more modest status accorded to the experimental sciences.

The problem is thornier and more especially crucial in a society, like France, that is a stalled society; this will be the underlying theme of this book. There is no lack of talk of change in a stalled society, but, in spite of revolutionary appearances, there is a complete refusal to envisage the slightest real change; one of the basic defenses of this sort of society is its capacity to mask or confuse reality. This major failing is still further aggravated as pressure for change grows; it is possible to show that French society was paradoxically far more aware of the mechanisms governing it in 1900 than it is today.*

Sociologists have suddenly begun to fascinate the French intellectual world in that, having assumed or having had thrust upon them an uncomfortable, Cassandra-like role, they became, by force of circumstance, objects of scandal. Their esoteric language and obscure debates suddenly seemed to hide a deeper meaning, like the biblical texts or passages from *Capital* over which earlier generations disputed in times of crisis. But this oracular role stifled the original contribution they might have made, and made it even harder to move beyond the prescientific tradition which had engulfed them.

The fact is that it is much harder than one thinks to state the problem of change in scientific terms. For one thing, sociolo-

* I shall deal further with this problem in Chapters 6 and 7, and especially in Chapter 9.

gists have not yet learned how to cope with the dimension of time. But more than that, they, like most intellectuals, are paralyzed by their own ambivalence, which makes them vacillate constantly between two opposing viewpoints: the determinist illusion, according to which the social mechanism leaves no room for human freedom; and the voluntarist illusion, which would have us believe that society is capable of reform in accordance with objectives it is free to fix as it sees fit.

The intellectual method every sociologist is finally obliged to adopt, a "functionalist" or "systemic" method, makes him very vulnerable to these opposite temptations. Essentially, it consists in revealing the interdependence of various elements in a particular system, and the various levels or stages of one and the same reality, and then in analyzing the system's mechanisms. By starting with this kind of reasoning, however, one develops a natural tendency both to exaggerate the determinism and, at the same time, to reject it in favor of out-and-out voluntarism.

On one level, for example, one on which Marxism operated to at least some extent, people are amazed by the contradictions they discover within the functionalist chain, and they immediately deduce that changes are imminent which will resolve these contradictions, as if all systems ineluctably tended toward harmony. The final crisis is expected to transform determinism's naturally catastrophic outlook into a completely voluntarist universe.

On another level, one on which a certain kind of American sociology still operates, people realize that far more profound interdependences underlie the apparent contradictions, but they go on to believe that these interdependences are far closer than they really are and to think that the deepest layer of reality—values—determines all the rest. If this were so, either one would have to admit that changes occur independently of human responsibility, or else dream that some kind of psychological action upon values, by transforming man through education, could automatically set in motion the transformation of the social system.

The heart of the problem lies in the implicit postulates that early scientific sociology unconsciously retained. In contrast to them, the scientific experience we have acquired has taught us:

1. Systems do not necessarily tend toward harmony. Conflicts and contradictions are an inseparable part of their functioning, are never resolved, but, rather, are eventually outlived and replaced by other conflicts and contradictions.

2. There is always a wide margin of tolerance among the various elements of a system or among the different levels of a single reality. Theoretically incompatible elements coexist in all the living systems known to us. The principle of coherence is no more a governing principle than is the principle of harmony.

3. If a change effected on one level of a system has repercussions on its overall functioning, then the bottommost level is not determinant; adjustments may occur at any point and at any level.

If we truly wish to state the problem of change in rational, i.e., experimental, terms, we must forget the enormous accumulation of scholastic glosses and begin with these empirical observations.

Two questions appear to be central:

1. How, under what conditions, and when do tensions that normally tend to strengthen a stable system become too difficult to maintain and begin to induce upheaval, breakdown, and eventually transformation?

2. How and within what limits do the members of a system learn rules other than the ones whose application naturally leads back to the traditional system? Are there social or institutional learning processes comparable to the individual learning processes demonstrated by psychologists? Under what conditions do they emerge?

Sociologists have already made a great deal of progress in exploring these questions at the small-group level. Where organizations are concerned, however, we still depend on comparative analyses. But these are beginning to mount up, and by checking them, comparing them, and studying what sort of generalizations we can make from them, we can go beyond the false debates that have trapped us for so long.

In this book I have applied this approach to a series of key issues facing post-industrial society, and thus analyzed the difficulties confronting French society and its possibilities for change. These reflections are based on a number of highly speculative hypotheses, and I would be the first to recognize that they have yet to be demonstrated. But their underlying logic is entirely different from traditional intellectual logic. My arguments are not based on intellectual coherence nor are they normative. Rather, they are drawn from experience in doing social surveys, the comparative format of which makes them early stand-ins for the plans of future experiments. Whatever their shortcomings, they have at least enabled us to bring about a regular confrontation with reality.

The reader will perhaps be surprised by the apparently optimistic tone of my account. The fact is that these surveys, and this confrontation, have led me to a far more favorable view of the real conditions of man's freedom and responsibility than is generally the case.

It may be that this is merely the consequence of a particular perspective. We are accustomed to musing about the constraints and dangers that lie ahead, and we often forget that the men who are going to have to suffer these constraints and confront these dangers will be very different from contemporary man. Similarly, the constraints of the past appear to us to have been slight, since we interpret them in the context of our current capacity for intellectual analysis; but they were extremely burdensome for those who had to support them—indeed, men in the past were very profoundly manipulated and exploited by means that would be powerless against us. We get a more optimistic, or at least less pessimistic, view of the future if we take into account our deformation of the object under analysis.

We are appalled when the social sciences reveal to us the infinite conditioning of our existence. Many young people reject everything, as a sort of defensive reaction to this, as though by suppressing knowledge they could eliminate conditioning. They have yet to learn that it is only through knowledge that they will win back their liberty. If a hasty study of sociology apparently condemns us to determinism, it is nonetheless through the development of a more authentic science that we shall become capable of living more freely.

PART ONE

THE TRANSFORMATION OF SOCIAL RELATIONS IN ADVANCED SOCIETIES

CHAPTER ONE

The Problem of Power

Any crisis that paves the way for or accompanies a profound change in society forces us to come to grips with the basic problem in all collective life: the problem of power.

In recent years protesters have focused on the problem of authority rather than on the problem of power.* But if authority—traditional or legal authority—were to be weakened, or even if it were to collapse, it does not necessarily follow that human relations would suddenly become free and transparent. The moment an old legitimacy, in which even its possessors have lost faith, is seriously challenged, new power phenomena begin to emerge that cannot be ignored without creating irresistible pressure for a return to the old forms.

For a long time the popularity of Marxism and the violence of the antagonisms it aroused prevented us from seeing the importance of this problem in a society that had already changed profoundly and was perhaps ripe for further change. In the heat of a more and more anachronistic debate—its terms of reference were all nineteenth-century ones—we let ourselves be

---

* I shall distinguish here between the problem of authority—any form of power recognized as legitimate by law, custom, or a sufficient consensus of those subject to it—and the problem of power in general, that is, all relationships between men characterized by the phenomena of dependence, manipulation, or exploitation.

carried away with the idea that the problem of power was secondary to more essential issues, such as those of property or development, of which it was no more than an instrument or justification. But the internal crisis that many of our institutions are now experiencing give us some idea of the primacy of problems of government in its broadest sense—the organization of power relationships among men.

The more we recognize the fragility of the old order based on nothing more than conventions, and thus discover how free we really are to create a new order, the more we are obliged to recognize that we cannot escape dealing with this problem, that we absolutely must try to find a means of regulating power relationships among people, and that all other problems are merely the conditions or consequences of this fundamental issue. Simplistic propositions and fanatical demands which blossom forth on all sides in the midst of the present crisis do not falsify this analysis if we see them for what they are: in the face of anxiety created by awareness of our freedom, they are panic responses and desperate attempts to rediscover the security of clear-cut distinctions.

Can the social sciences enable us to deal more positively with the disturbing problem of power? They too are profoundly marked by the customs and taboos of an era when a great deal of time was spent trying to avoid the issue. But it is only in their terms, and through their renewal, that we can identify and state the problem of power in its entirety. Above all, it is through work now being done by social scientists that we can assess the kinds of progress made possible by evolution, and judge man's capacity to develop better arrangements for dealing with power in the future.

The Social-Science Difficulties

The concept of power is central to the social sciences. Phenomena of power always accompany all processes of social integration, and these are one of the subjects, if not the essential subject, of study in sociology. One might even say that, without power, neither integration nor society is possible. But since the social sciences are not very fully developed, and consequently reflect very closely the prejudices of their time, they are ill prepared to use this kind of concept effectively.

The concept of power is, in fact, extremely difficult to deal with. It is too vague and too ambiguous, and it too easily explains too many problems. Worse, it is difficult to clarify it, since its imprecision and the contradictions it raises stem not from the uncertainty of the word "power" but from the ambiguity of the facts of power themselves.

Sociologists and political scientists have long been wary of difficulties of this kind. Empirically oriented sociologists, influenced by a rather narrow kind of scientism, have nearly always claimed that they disregard phenomena that are too imprecise or that cannot be quantified; they study the determinants of attitudes and behavior as though the only kinds of relationship that existed between people were formal ones, or phenomena of spontaneous attraction. The more classical, humanist sociologists would seem, on the contrary, to have projected the systematic interpretive schemas they could not develop elsewhere onto this confused subject; hence the flowering of conspiracy theories of power (such as that of C. Wright Mills), and theories of the absence or universal distribution of power. But fascination with power as a myth turns out to be no more constructive than the empiricists' neglect. Withal, the two attitudes would appear complementary.

To get over these contradictions, one must squarely face a spot that all the perfumes of our ideological Arabias cannot sweeten: no concrete relationship between either individuals or groups is free of issues of power.

In the last few years social scientists have made some progress here. We are gradually learning to approach the issue experimentally, thanks in part to the development of new disciplines like decision-making theory and games theory, and to the influence they have had on political science and sociology, and in part to greater empirical understanding of the sociology of organizations. Here the theoretical and empirical efforts join in trying to state the problems of government in concrete, if not yet operational, terms. But the new approach nonetheless raises several important questions. The awkwardness and contradictions surrounding power phenomena can only be dissipated gradually, and this is so for three very different reasons: moral, logical, and methodological.

From the moral point of view, it is still very hard to rid ourselves of all the moral taboos that have grown up around this subject. Everyone claims to be liberated in this respect, but this freedom is usually no more than a suppression of the problem. The taboo about power is still perhaps more profoundly rooted in the conscience of modern man than the taboo about sex. The right-thinking modern intellectual, who is horrified when one speaks of sexual behavior in terms of good and evil, is deeply shocked by any scientific analysis of relations of dependence or domination. For him, and for most of us, domination and dependence are moral categories, not facts.

From the point of view of logic, power phenomena, because they are integrative, arise naturally from contradictory and at first view irreconcilable modes of reasoning. To understand them one must pursue both a rational, instrumental analysis of the classic type and an affective type of analysis at the same time. Indeed, power can be conceived only in an ends-oriented perspective, which suggests that the power game must always conform, in one way or another, to rational rules based on efficiency; but at the same time it arouses some extremely strong affective reactions, so that the play of power is also conditioned by the capacity of individuals to withstand these reactions.

Lastly, from a structural point of view, no power relationship can be dissociated from the institutional system or systems within which it develops. There can be no neutral field. Each power relationship is shaped by a whole series of "structural" constraints that condition the rules of the game, and it therefore expresses, at a secondary level, the logic of the institutions or structures. However autonomous it may be, it cannot change substantially without deeply affecting the system of which it is an integral part.

Faced with these obstacles, social scientists have too often let their work dwindle into description or only partial analysis. For example, they will make distinctions among types of power according to the way it is exercised: power based on coercion, power based on the distribution of rewards or on mechanisms of identification, power based on expertise, and legitimate power. This way of going about it may be useful as a start, but it immediately stumbles on a huge block: it gives us no help in understanding how different types of power are reconciled and how arbitration between them operates. The principal virtue of power as an integrative phenomenon is that it is susceptible to confrontation, transfer, and exchange. If one claims that forms of power coming from different sources have nothing in common and cannot be compared, then it is impossible to understand or predict how, in reality, they are brought together and how they balance each other out. Let us take an example. The legitimate power a mayor has over the municipal employees subordinate to him is clearly completely different from the kind of power that private interests who could bribe them, or the network of relationships they depend on to do their work efficiently, may have over these same employees. Obviously, these various forms of power exercised over the same group of people are different in kind, and it is important not to confuse them. We must distinguish clearly between them and even oppose them for analytical purposes. But it is also essential that we discover their common denominator in order to understand the results of their interaction.

We must therefore go beyond the descriptive approach, which is mainly of taxonomic interest, in order, if possible, to lay the empirical foundations of a "strategic" analysis that will enable us to assess the opposing forces and to uncover the laws governing their interaction and reconciliation.

This can be achieved, I believe—or at least we can make a start—if we no longer consider power solely from the viewpoint of a "wielder" of power, but look on it rather as a relationship between individuals or groups, as a process developing over time that, with its goals and its rules of play, affects the organization or system within which the various parties act (or which they have formed for the purpose).

Power as a Relationship and as a Process

Any kind of power, whatever its sources, its legitimacy, objectives, and means whereby it is exercised, implies the possibility of action by an individual or group on one or more other individuals or groups. This is what Robert Dahl wanted to make clear when he proposed his famous, oft-quoted definition: The power of A over B is the capacity of A to make B do something he would not have done without the intervention of A.

The main virtue of a definition like this is its simplicity. It has the advantage that it does not require as a prerequisite any theory about the essence of power, it is equally applicable to all forms of power, and it makes power amenable to some sort of measurement. But if one wants to use it operationally, it presents some difficulties.

In the first place, it does not really enable us to distinguish between power as an intentional, conscious relationship, which implies a confrontation between two parties, and power as an involuntary influence that one actor may exert over another without either of them necessarily being aware of it. Clearly we can speak of power in both cases, but equally clearly we are not speaking about the same thing.

In the second place, precise measurement is not very likely, since A's capacity to exercise power over B varies, depending on the action demanded, and experience shows that there is no standard of measurement. Each "power relation" is specific: A can make B do *a*, whereas X, who cannot make B do this, can, on the other hand, get him to do *b*, which A couldn't possibly manage.

Lastly, and most important, experience has shown us that a "power relation" is not only specific but also reciprocal; if A can make B do something he would not have done otherwise, it is quite likely that B, for his part, is capable of making A do something he would not have done without B's intervention.

These difficulties need not stop us from using Dahl's definition, but they do limit its applicability to relatively vague comparisons bearing solely on the capacities of each individual as a wielder of power. This kind of comparison lets us emphasize the universal and interchangeable nature of power relations, but it tells us little about the way they work.

If we take a look now, not at power in the sense of the individual capacities of A and B, but at the power that develops in relations between the two parties A and B, we discover a bargaining element that completely alters the meaning of the thing. Any relationship between two parties requires a measure of exchange and mutual adjustment. Any positive response by A to a request by B may clearly be considered to be the consequence of B's power over A. But it is simpler, and more fruitful, to look at it rather as the result of negotiation. A responds to B's demands because B has responded to A's, or else because A thinks B will respond to him. If the two parties are completely free and if the exchange is equal, one cannot really talk in terms of power. But if the balance of the exchange is tipped one way or the other, and if this inequality corresponds to the respective situations of the two parties and is not the result of chance or an error on the part of one of them, then we can speak of a power relationship. We could then justifiably say, somewhat altering Dahl's original statement, that A's power over B corresponds to A's capacity to impose on B terms of exchange that are favorable to A.

If one accepts this new formulation, the essential problem of power is no longer that of the capacity for command or action, but the more precise and limited problem of conditions governing interaction between partners.

At first sight it might seem as though the relative strength of the two parties—the balance of power—would naturally determine the outcome. But this proposition has no operational value, since strength and balance of power are meaningful only in terms of the relationship itself. Strong people are not strong in the abstract. They must be both willing and able to exercise their strength. In a situation where the use of force or wealth is either forbidden or impossible, the weak and poor can prevail over the rich and strong; the balance of power thus becomes the balance of pertinent and usable power.

The analysis is now somewhat more precise, but it is still inadequate, for it tells us nothing about the nature of the forces or about the players' strategy. Strength and power cannot be accumulated like war chests. If we observe the players closely, we see that the key to their behavior lies in the margin of freedom and maneuver they can secure for themselves. A confrontation between partners is not a trial of strength but an exchange of possibilities of action. Let us take the rare but not unusual case of a powerful executive who is restricted when dealing with a weak subordinate to a single possible course of action, while the subordinate can choose among several. The executive will have nothing to exchange and will be in an inferior position vis-à-vis the subordinate—who can, if he keeps a cool head, cause his superior serious difficulties. The more one can affect one's partner's situation by using one's freedom of maneuver, the less vulnerable one is before him and the more power one has over him. The game consists, then, in trying to force the other player into a determinate pattern of behavior while at the same time staying free enough oneself to be able to make him pay for one's good will. The balance of power is a confrontation between the partners' respective abilities to keep their future behavior less predictable. Strength, wealth, prestige, legitimate authority are influential only insofar as they give their possessors greater freedom of action.

In the context of a simple bargaining relationship, however, notions of freedom of action and predictability of behavior are vague. They can be made more precise only if we put this relationship in its natural context, i.e., a more or less structured system with its own manifest and latent objectives and its own rules.

Power does not exist in a vacuum. A power relation can develop only if the two parties are already part of, or choose to participate in, an organized system, however temporarily. Two strangers meeting on a train do not find themselves in a power situation, regardless of any cultural differences or inequalities in strength or wealth. But the moment circumstances join them together in a common undertaking, the negotiations they are implicitly forced to engage in will reveal the development of a power relationship, the start of an organization. The terms of exchange and the conditions of the negotiation are in fact profoundly linked to their joint enterprise, and in a certain sense express it. Power requires organization. Men can attain their collective ends only through the exercise of power relationships, but, conversely, they can exercise power over each other only when pursuing these collective ends, which directly condition their bargaining activities.

To understand the basic elements and dynamics of power negotiations, one must focus on the overall organization serving as their framework. Power then appears no longer merely as a relationship but as a process inseparable from the organizational process. The terms of the exchange result neither from chance nor from some abstract and theoretical balance of power. They are the result of a game whose constraints create compulsory hurdles and opportunities for manipulation for the players, and therefore determine their strategy.

What are these constraints? Basically, they are the formal and informal objectives laid down by the organization and accepted by the participants, as well as the rules imposed on them or established by them. We should emphasize that these objectives and these rules do not work directly. Their principal role is indirect: by limiting the players' freedom of action they will establish sectors where actions are entirely predictable, and others where uncertainty is dominant.

In negotiating with the organization, a player's power ultimately depends on the control he has over a source of uncertainty that affects the pursuit of the organization's aims, and on the importance of this source as compared with other relevant sources. In negotiating with another player, his power depends on the control he can exercise over a source of uncertainty affecting this other player's behavior within the context of the rules imposed by the organization.

To go further, we must resort to case-study analyses. To measure one individual's power over another, one must analyze the sources of uncertainty each controls within the organization they belong to, the respective importance of these uncertainties to the organization's objectives, and the limitations imposed on both players by the rules they must obey in order to continue playing. We have come a long way from the usual mechanical models and those famously clever but contradictory axioms about power ("The more one demonstrates power, the more one acquires it"; "The more one exercises one's power, the weaker it becomes"), yet this institutional approach precludes neither the measurement of phenomena nor the search for more general laws. However, insistence on putting them into a structural study makes such attempts extremely difficult. In particular, the problem of rules constitutes a preliminary problem that cannot easily be resolved.

The Two Faces of Power

Each participant in an organization, in an organized system, or even in society as a whole, wields power over the system he belongs to and over the members of this system, insofar as he occupies a strategically favorable position as regards the problems on which the success of the system depends. But at the same time his power is limited by the rules of the game, which restrict the use he can make of his advantages.

However, while it may be natural enough to begin by separately studying, first, the mechanism of power relationships arising out of the explicit and implicit bargains that individuals strike between themselves and with the organization, and, second, the rules preventing the players from using their advantages beyond a certain point, an analysis more attentive to reality would lead us to look on the second factor, the rules themselves, as a crystallization of other power relationships and the results of earlier negotiations which may have been less explicit but were every bit as real. The rules of the game tend, in effect, to demarcate artificial sources of uncertainty, enabling those who control them to negotiate on better terms with players whose favorable strategic situation otherwise puts them in a position of superiority. Moreover, the rules can develop and gain acceptance only because another source of uncertainty, more important than all the others—namely, the question of the survival of the entire organization—binds all its members.

This analysis may seem unduly formal, but it serves the important purpose of highlighting two contradictory aspects of power that are indissolubly linked together. On one hand, the power relationship appears as something inadmissible and shameful—quite simply, as blackmail. On the other hand, power is honored as the legitimate, necessary, and respectable expression of the social control that is vital to the success of any collective effort. It might be argued that this contrast is unwarranted and depends on an arbitrarily extensive definition of power. But this objection will not stand up to close scrutiny, for the official pyramid of power cannot operate without recourse to blackmail, while in all informal negotiations based on blackmail, social constraints, the general interest, and the primacy of collective goals still have some part to play.

Let us take the example of the relations between superiors and subordinates within an organization. The superior has the right to give certain orders to his subordinates, while the latters' duty is to obey these orders. This relationship is highly valued, and it retains a moral connotation, in our vocabulary at least: we still speak of the *duty* to obey, and we are still morally shocked by insubordination, which we can explain only in terms of moral failing on the part of one or the other of the protagonists. On the other hand, if the superior uses his pre-eminence to obtain something from his subordinates that is not provided for in the rules, we then speak of an abuse of power. In reality, however, the two go together. Subordinates are in a position to exert a great deal of pressure on their boss, since his success in an organization ultimately depends on their zeal and good will. He can respond to these pressures only by "abusing" his power. He must, in order to retain sufficient freedom of maneuver, threaten to apply the rules strictly and, conversely, make it understood that he will tolerate substantial stretching of the rules in exchange for good behavior; if he depended solely on his legitimate power, he would quickly find himself powerless. In contrast, the expert who knows that he is irreplaceable and who could theoretically, therefore, blackmail the organization into accepting almost anything, can use only official procedures and must make it clear that he subscribes to the common goals of the organization. He cannot succeed in manipulating the organization unless he lets himself be manipulated by it. In both cases, the shameful and the noble faces of power are inextricably bound together. Blackmail is employed for lofty ends, and noble power serves as a screen for blackmail operations.

I have wittingly used moral terms here because common sense and sociology are agreed that moral judgments are definitely involved: power is good and noble if it corresponds to the officially accepted social pact; it is reprehensible and immoral if it is used as a means to take advantage of one's situation in order to manipulate others outside the recognized pact. But experience makes it clear that moral judgments of this kind are contradictory, for power in its noble aspect arises out of dubious negotiations and has to rely on blackmail in its exercise. The established order of things is merely the ratified outcome of prior relationships in which blackmail played a major role. On what grounds can we condemn present blackmail in the name of past blackmail? It is impossible to eliminate blackmail anyway, since it is related to the perennial need for adjustment and innovation. No human enterprise can adapt to its environment if it is reduced to its formal power, to the theoretical pact which defines it.

As is frequently the case in such matters, judgments become more violent as the distinction between good and evil becomes more dubious. This may be one of the reasons why the concept of power remains so ambiguous, and why sociologists have such difficulty using it.

All the same, the critique made by traditional morals would be of little interest if it did not reveal the function of this moralism and how it can be overcome. The value we attribute to power in the noble sense of the term derives, I believe, from the fact that all collective human undertakings have great difficulty in gaining the adherence and conformity of their participants. To impose the priority of collective goals over individual claims, the latter have to be considered morally reprehensible, while the official hierarchic power is, in contrast, exalted as the guardian of the collective goal. Negotiation is suppressed if it threatens to jeopardize the organized system that most of the participants believe to be indispensable, and moral or religious reasoning is invoked instead. Of course, even moral discussion involves pressures and counterpressures; we speak, for example, of a fair wage, and of the necessary prerogatives of the leader. Only little by little can the real nature of human relations be talked about openly, as people become readier to understand and accept the disciplines necessary to collective action. I would like to argue that the major trend in organizational practice over the past hundred years has been one from the rule of morality to the rule of negotiation.

If we can extrapolate from the experience of organizations to the functioning of broader, less structured entities, we can say that this gradually emerging consciousness on the part of societies constitutes a new kind of coming of age, comparable to earlier awakenings concerning, for example, anthropocentrism and ethnocentrism.

The clearest example of this evolution, and the one easiest to acknowledge because it has been established for so long, is the recognition of the right to strike. Few people now recall that strikes were once considered an unthinkable form of blackmail and that they only gradually came to be accepted as a legitimate form of the power to negotiate. This evolution is far from complete, but we can clearly see the direction it is taking.

The gradual recognition of reality and of the legitimacy of each participant's use of his advantages in collective life is a sign of greater maturity among individuals and of their organizational capacities in a given society. But at the same time it completely alters the conditions of collective action. The impulses which before could be expressed only in contradictions and paralysis of bureaucracies or hierarchies, in religious and social taboos, can now be resolved more rapidly and efficiently. Hierarchical power need not depend so much on constraint and can divest itself of its problematical moral attributes in favor of greater flexibility and effectiveness, playing the less prestigious role of inspirer and facilitator.

This is a very different kind of evolution from what is hoped for in anarchist and revolutionary demands for the withering away of power. The general acceptance of open negotiation does not signify the elimination of power; on the contrary, it implies the rational acceptance of all *de facto* powers. It tends to reintegrate formerly shameful practices into the field of legitimate human relationships. It may seem paradoxical to view the disappearance of the traditional dichotomy between the official, rigid world of the formal hierarchy and the darker world of secret dealings as progress. But this change of perspective enables us to make human relations more wholesome in the same way that the rehabilitation of man's repressed drives by psychoanalysis helps him to be more free and more responsible. At the same time, shameful power practices become less so when legitimate power loses its halo of nobility and when society, recognizing the pressures arising out of the natural interaction of its members, makes it easier for them to participate in the achievement of society's goals. Change becomes natural, and innovation is encouraged.

Power in the Social System

These few remarks concerning power as a social process, as a condition, and as an expression of all organized activity do not, of course, permit us to make any conclusions about the government of a social system. Nevertheless, they highlight a few basic points concerning the general evolution of power relationships in modern industrial and post-industrial societies.

Problems of power in society as a whole are not so simple as those in an organization. We have to deal with relationships on another level, carried on between organizations, each having a specific rationale, far more determinate and settled than the rationality of the system within which their negotiations take place. Moreover, the games played by individuals, organizations, and society as a whole tend to overlap and coincide. Society can influence organizations through the pressure of individuals. And this brings us to the concept of influence, which we have so far ignored in our discussion of organizations, but which is decisively important here. It is through this type of power—unconscious, nonnegotiated influence—that social control is exercised and that the rules of play permitting society as a whole to continue functioning are imposed, in the face of divergent pressures from all the different interests at stake.

These differences and oppositions do not, however, completely transform the situation. The rules we have established concerning the necessary link between all power relations and the beginning of an organized system with shared objectives and rules also apply to society as a whole. Negotiations in society are not free, nor do they correspond to any mechanical application of the balance of power. Rather, the balance of power depends essentially on constraints affecting all the parties involved and reflecting their relative dependence in society as a whole. As is the case within an organization, each party tries to manipulate this relationship by using what mastery it has over the sources of uncertainty affecting the other party's behavior, at the same time respecting the commonly accepted rules and objectives. The most important difference is that the counter-vailing power, the social control governing the whole, is not very formalized or constraining and must use much more indirect means. But a high moral value is placed on it all the same, and if most of the time it cannot capitalize on the entire society's need to survive, it can nonetheless, in such extreme cases as war, appeal to this necessity.

These likenesses are becoming more and more important in the modern world, as the result of a double movement that is bringing organizations and society closer together. On one hand, the fact that organizations are evolving toward more open and tolerant forms of human relationships is tending to transform them into "political societies." On the other hand, society as a whole is giving rise to organized subsystems, within which social control is expressed through more and more conscious decisions.

These two convergent phenomena may appear incompatible: more tolerance on one side, increasing rigor on the other. But at a deeper level they reflect the same evolution. We try to integrate into the formal decision-making procedure those unacknowledged negotiations which accompany and paralyze it. We also seek to substitute organized systems, which allow fully conscious decisions, for the blind conflict of interests, which can take no account of secondary consequences. The effort is being made in a number of realms, but on both sides the approach is much the same—people are realizing the complexity of action—and so is the objective: to broaden the accepted range of forces at play so that we can openly (and contradictorily) take into account both the interests and the strategic positions bearing on the situation, as well as the general interest of the surrounding milieu.

In the case of society as a whole, we are concerned not with the integration of a hidden world whose existence has hitherto been denied, but with bridging the deep chasm that separated the world of interests from the world of formal or moral decisions. The clearest aspect of this change—the recognition of the importance of interests in formal or moral decisions, and official consultation between powers whose concealed blackmail had hitherto been considered immoral—stems from precisely the same inspiration we have already noted in organizations. In both instances we have become more acutely aware of the conditions under which human beings participate in the collective enterprise, and we have a new, more tolerant vision of the relationship between the two faces—moral and immoral, noble and ignoble—of power. Moralization, tolerance, and rationalization go hand in hand.

One final problem remains to be dealt with, however—that of the general interest. We know that the general interest does not arise from the confrontation of all interests taken together, and that tolerance and acceptance of all those inadmissible pressures are not enough to produce a "general interest." Something more is needed, whereby the whole becomes more than the sum of its parts. In the case of an organization, the power corresponding to this need is attached to its leadership, which affirms it by using the uncertainty affecting all the members concerning the survival of the organization and their continued membership in it. In the case of society as a whole, no equivalent criterion enables us clearly to assess the general interest.

Hence the high moral value placed on politics, and the persistence of an unavoidable imperative factor. In the first place, a state policy is the outcome of the play between diverse influences affecting individuals and the resulting consensus on one hand, and on the other the pressures of all existing powers; but, in the second place, it depends on contingent choices made above and beyond this by leaders in strategic positions. In the dialogue between the leaders and the mass of society's members concerning the use the leaders make of the arbitrary power necessarily left in their hands, the general interest can evolve from the metaphysical to the rational plane. This transformation is only now becoming possible. But its accomplishment depends far less on progress made in the conception or ideology of the general interest than it does on a healthy interplay of power relations. We cannot deal rationally with the irreducible element of freedom so long as we have failed to rationalize and moralize the preponderant element of functioning and constraint that conditions all activity.

CHAPTER TWO

The Problem of Innovation

For a long time men have discussed the social order, and the possible modes of government of human groups, without considering the problem raised by the *evolution* of these groups and especially by the emergence and success of innovations within them. The theme of innovations was raised in the nineteenth century during debates over the economic system, but, characteristically, it was introduced against traditionalist and Marxist arguments in order to justify the entrepreneur's function; it was not considered as an independent problem.

The acceleration of change we are currently experiencing (or perhaps we should say from which we are benefiting) makes it important that we start treating this as a practical problem, for its resolution may well determine the success and survival of post-industrial society.

Until now the subject of innovation has been almost exclusively a concern of economists, statisticians, and certain psychologists. It has been related only very indirectly to problems of society and government. For example, people generally tend to keep the study of the laws of technological progress strictly separated from the study of human phenomena accompanying such progress. Economists and statisticians analyzed the characteristics of scientific investment and the rate of technological innovation, while psychologists and sociologists studied how individuals and groups resist change, or the psychological conditions under which a discovery is made public and disseminated. But, while acceleration of technological progress and newly fierce economic competition give us a better insight into the overall reasons for success or failure in innovation, they also tend to show how artificial this separation is.

The human problems attendant upon technological innovation are not confined to passive resistance in the lower echelons of the work force, or to the psychology of the entrepreneur; they exist on all levels and express a whole range of difficulties. Technical progress and human relations are intimately related. What we have to examine is the capacity for innovation in the system as a whole, and this depends just as much on the way the system is governed as on its finances or its level of intellectual development.

This matter of innovation goes way beyond the older issues—economic growth, welfare, and the consumer society— to which we were slowly becoming accustomed. What is now at stake is the creative capacity of individuals and of society—a capacity which we are beginning to understand in the economic field, but which is involved in other realms as well.

This creative capacity should not be seen as a by-product or condition of either stability or economic growth. In some ways it is at the very heart of human relations and collective living. It is understood increasingly as one of the fundamental needs of advanced society, as well as one of the criteria by which society will ultimately be judged. But, like the concept of power, the concept of innovation is problematic, and people are reluctant to tackle it because, like all integrative concepts, it is confused and contradictory at first sight. Like the concept of power, it must be understood in terms of both the instrumental logic of economics and the affective logic of human relationships—both of these being conditioned by a third logic, which derives from the structure of the hierarchized groups within which the human relations occur.

But the questions raised by innovation are very different from those which have inhibited our thinking on power. In the first place, the powerful influence of economic reasoning on the issue of innovation makes it difficult to take affective and structural dimensions into account. And classical economic theory further hampers us by treating the entrepreneur as the central, if not the only person involved in innovation, reducing the innovative process to a question of market forces.

To see all this in perspective, it is worth restating in sociological terms the reasoning underlying the classical economic analysis of innovation.

The Theory and Practice of Innovation in the Classical Market System

The postulates of an "entrepreneur" and a "market" were indispensable to classical economic models, but they have little meaning outside the instrumental logic used in economics. If we transpose them intact to the field of sociology, they help us to understand neither the conditions under which the entrepreneurial spirit emerges, nor the role of the individual (entrepreneur and nonentrepreneur) in the process of innovation, nor the practical problems that all innovations pose.

Let us start with the problem of innovation in the nineteenth-century context, when the entrepreneurial figure corresponded to a fairly specific sociological reality. Even here, an analysis of business practices will demonstrate that the entrepreneur's innovative actions conformed only very imperfectly to market rationale. Unexploited inventions, the continued use of out-moded techniques, commercial risks not taken—there is any amount of evidence of how difficult and how rare it was to innovate. Why was this? Undoubtedly it was partly because entrepreneurs lacked motivation, but it was also because of institutional constraints and the responses of a social system that opposed change. The relation between the entrepreneur and his environment is not only one of economic rationality but also a sociological matter. The entrepreneur's actions are determined in part by his position in the social system, by the rules of the game in the milieu or subsystem he belongs to, and by the values which express these aspects of his social life.

Why, how, and in what way do these values and rules inhibit or foster innovations?

Let us look more closely at the person we call the entrepreneur. First and foremost he is an overseer, controller, and employer of workmen, whose skill at organizing is indispensable to the production of certain goods. From this function, which is a difficult one to perform, he derives profit and, eventually, prestige. His gain is an individual one and it depends on the market, but it also derives from a sort of collective recognition, amounting to influence, coming from other members of the same group of entrepreneurs having monopolized the same function.

This influence is a traditional phenomenon, and the group naturally tries to protect it. As a result, a deep solidarity unites the group, despite the competition among its members. It is a matter of maintaining standards in the profession, restricting access to it, and preventing its exercise from becoming easy or even simply widely known. These inevitable reactions are not necessarily opposed to innovation, but at first glance innovation is a risk. It may jeopardize the group's position in society, and in any event it threatens its internal hierarchy, its internal relationships, and some of its capacities for action. Caste systems and guilds gave legalized form to these needs of the group, and, while the nineteenth-century market and free-enterprise system removed their legal sanctions, the group demands endured and were expressed through other forms: through public opinion, restrictive regulations, government intervention, pressure from the workers, the banking system, the transport system, the distribution system.

The mechanism for innovation in such a system is characterized by the large gap that exists between its ideal of market rationality and its actually very restrictive social practices. One may understand this sociologically as a series of oppositions between groups and society, between the individual and his group, and even within the individual himself. The group is always and inevitably conservative, and the individual must be responsible for innovation. He has to develop it against the group, which will use all available means to slow him down, primarily by branding his behavior as unfair and illegitimate.

This group pressure induces a certain internal contradiction within the individual members, where not only values are concerned (progressive values conflicting with conservative ones and ones based on respect for the others) but rational calculation as well. The entrepreneur, looking for innovations that will give him a decisive advantage over his competitors, at the same time always hesitates before taking the plunge, since he knows that the rules of the game generally tend to penalize the first in any field. Once successful, on the other hand, the innovator does not want to eliminate the obstacles that have hurt him, since the rewards he is hoping for depend, in this system, on the preservation of them. The successful innovator tends to become conservative even in the development of his own innovation.

These same antagonisms can also be seen in society as a whole, where the combined pressure of conservative groups tends to restrain the rationalizing pressure of the mass of society acting through legal institutions, educational establishments, et cetera.

Finally, innovation is easiest to come by in the least prestigious activities, carried on by the most marginal groups. In the best-organized activities and most traditional groups, competition tends to be transferred to the least dangerous (the most formal) aspects of the functions fulfilled. So it is not true that competition necessarily leads to innovation. In the mandarinate of old China, for example, there may have been perfect competition between individuals for public office, but there was no chance of its leading to the slightest innovation.

These difficulties, pressures, and contradictions among groups and within individuals make themselves manifest by an atmosphere of secrecy and isolation. This isolation makes collaboration very uncertain—between scientists and practitioners, between inventors and manufacturers, and, more generally, among the people with the expertise needed to achieve a new synthesis, which is what any innovation is.

When a new secret can finally be put to use by the few people who are intellectually and socially capable of exploiting it, innovation finally wins through, but it can for a long time continue in a state of secrecy, paying a royalty to those who appropriated it. On the other hand, if the exploitation of the innovation creates too great an imbalance for the business, a crisis is likely to occur, as a result of which the innovation will quickly be generalized.

Only emergency situations make it possible to avoid the clumsiness of these processes (or at least make it possible to speed them up)—which is why war plays a remarkably positive role in the process of innovation.

Innovation in a System Dominated by Large Organizations

To those who continue to interpret the classical schema narrowly, it will seem obvious that our present-day system, dominated by large organizations, ought to be less favorable to innovation than the nineteenth-century market system, with its mass of theoretically equal entrepreneurs. The success of large organizations reduces the number of units capable of taking initiative and tends to regulate and restrict, if not to stifle, competition.

Experience has shown, however, that, on the contrary, the rhythm of change has accelerated amazingly and we are experiencing an explosion of innovations. If the very large organizations are not necessarily responsible for the most spectacular of these, the most rapid progress nonetheless occurs in those societies (and within them in those sectors) where large organization dominates.

The large-organization system is not, then, as we had long

supposed, necessarily inimical to change and innovation. Why is this? It is because the sociological mechanisms whose effects we have just discussed in the case of a classical market can be changed in a positive way when society moves to a large-organization system. Innovation is not merely an individual phenomenon, determined by strict economic rationality, but a collective system whose success depends on human factors as well, and here one large organization may well prove superior to many small producers.

Let us consider the problem from a practical point of view. The collective aspect of innovation can be seen at both ends of the decision to innovate. At the start, it is a question of bringing together all the resources needed for the new synthesis, the new product. These resources are always known to and controlled by different men or groups, and to obtain them one must negotiate and cooperate, or, rather, make these different groups negotiate and cooperate. So the whole problem becomes one of human relations—which, as we have seen, is not really resolved in the market system. At the other end of the decision to innovate is a question of the human consequences of the innovation. All too often, the difficulties arising from an innovation are taken into account only after the event. But more or less conscious apprehensions of them are bound to influence the initial decision, if only because they make it that much harder to mobilize the necessary resources.

When dealing with these issues, classical economists frequently saw, and see, nothing more than the one individual we call the entrepreneur. This simplification stands in the way of any attempt to understand the real conditions governing the success of a business. For an individual working in a traditional society's climate of secrecy and resistance, competition will only very partially push things along in the right direction. A large organization, on the other hand, if it is flexible enough, may offer more competitive situations within it—situations with fairly considerable possibilities for synthesis—not to mention better sources of information and better contacts. Finally, it is often better equipped to foresee and deal with certain consequences of activities. Thus it may well be better placed to innovate than the individual entrepreneurs it superseded.

But, someone may say, big organizations always become bureaucratic and heavy, stifling their members' creativity. I personally do not believe this is inevitable, but it is true that a large organization can continue to innovate only under certain conditions, and these depend on the principles by which it is managed and operated. The problem facing advanced societies, therefore, is to develop large organizations along with "democratic" forms of government and human relations that will enable them both to foster individual creativity and to channel it in the direction of collective innovation.

The first and essential condition for this is the preservation and development of freedom for individual initiative. The classical entrepreneur in theory enjoys unlimited freedom, but in practice his freedom is severely constricted because he belongs to a variety of profoundly conservative groups which, while they provide him with much needed psychological, moral, and social protection, are bound to clash with him if he wishes to innovate. Large organizations succeed when they can replace—at least on some levels—this paralyzing opposition with less problematic forms of participation. For this to occur, individuals must feel completely free in their relations to the organization; they must feel capable of leaving it from one day to the next without the slightest hesitation. This requirement may seem incompatible with the running of a complex business, yet it is found in the most dynamic fields of activity in the most advanced Western societies. In management and among all those engineers and scientists whose work is so important to innovation, the rate of turnover is very high indeed, yet the capacity of the businesses they work for to develop further seems in no way jeopardized.

The advantages of this, from the point of view of innovation, are obvious. When an innovation is planned, the key men involved are no longer inhibited by fear that their personal careers may suffer from contributing to it; at the same time they lose the desire—so paralyzing for their colleagues—to appropriate all possible profits accruing from an invention to their exclusive use. And the organization benefits from the close contacts it can now freely maintain with scientific and research communities. Exchanges will occur that not only broaden the intellectual horizons of individuals in the organization but make them more cooperative and mobilize underutilized resources.

But can an organization preserve its cohesion and efficiency in these circumstances?

Of course this is a very difficult problem, and Western societies—not to mention socialist societies—differ widely on this point, as much because of their differing cultures as because of their different degrees of technical and economic development. To resolve it, we are going to have to develop new models of human relationships that will reconcile very broad individual liberties with participation in a strictly controlled collective enterprise. We are now in the process of developing these models, and there is no reason to believe that this kind of learning process cannot be generalized. And success can be achieved in a great many different ways.

In the West, it should be noted, our models are still deeply marked by the classical model of competition—which is still flourishing vigorously, notwithstanding the changed context. This classical model is now operating on two different, apparently contradictory, levels. On one hand, competition between corporations seems to be essential, since it enables the organization, which takes full responsibility for a risk when the stakes are very high, to exercise strong pressure on the people who have agreed to become members of it. On the other hand, the competition enables individuals to exercise a great deal of pressure on the organization, insofar as they can easily offer their services to other organizations and no one will construe this as disloyalty.

These increased powers on both sides are, contrary to what was thought in the past, wholly compatible; the negotiations they necessitate are rather more complicated but at the same time more open and more fruitful. Mutual recognition of the opposing party's powers is a vital prerequisite for people learning to behave according to the new institutional model.

Institutional Problems Caused by Innovation

The first problem created by innovation in the post-industrial age concerns the internal management of organizations.

To begin with, organizations must assume their responsibilities concerning innovation. Now a modern organization's capacity for innovation, as I have tried to demonstrate, depends primarily on having rules that reward cooperative, constructive, and innovative activities instead of activities aimed at ensuring stability, harmony, and conservation. These rules express the system of government developed by the real power structure in the organization. In other words, no measure of formal democracy, no form of legally enforced participation, can promote a climate favorable to innovation; this can only depend upon a thoroughgoing transformation of the power relationships in question. This transformation in turn depends largely on socio-cultural factors: the degree to which people can tolerate conflict, their behavior toward authority roles, their capacity for cooperation. Organizations tend to change to the degree that, technical factors permitting, our improved understanding of them allows for greater risks (for example, when constraint is replaced with forecasting), and to the degree that the rules of the overall socio-economic system encourage innovating leaders to take risks themselves, by launching new experiments.

This evolution is not, of course, entirely automatic. Two types of deviation occur regularly. One forces management to centralize all decision-making, which results in a narrowly rational model of functioning and naturally restricts the capacity of the system to experiment and innovate. The other forces management to yield to pressure from subordinate groups demanding formal guarantees in opposed but complementary ways, as a consequence of which the system is blocked by a kind of democracy based on seniority; this deviation is equally inimical to innovation.

These two deviations arise from a common desire to destroy competition among individuals and groups within the organization. But neither the autocratic, centralizing solution nor the pseudo-democratic solution can do this. They merely direct the competition into channels still less favorable to innovation. Progress consists in recognizing that one simply cannot eliminate competition, but that one can channel it so that the judgments or choices sanctioning the activities of participants are essentially concerned with problems of efficiency and are capable of rewarding innovation.

At the present time the West is witnessing constant, though sometimes difficult and often thwarted, progress in this direction. The most important obstacle is still the fact that everyone affected by the process in which he is participating wants security. Actually, an overly categorical view of human possibilities in this matter would be dangerous, since the pace of progress has to be rather slow. After all, the structure has to retain a certain rigidity in order to protect individuals from the consequences of their errors and inadequacies. A process that was too open and brutal would be unbearable.

The second problem raised by innovation concerns noneconomic activities. These activities become more and more important as it becomes harder and harder to control the human and social consequences of the acceleration of change, and as we come to realize that it is on this ground, so very different from classical productive activities, that the battle for development is being fought.

Some noneconomic activities are partially dealt with within economic organizations. One of the great advantages of large modern organizations is that they can anticipate the consequences of their decisions. Their capacity for innovation increases to the extent that they are better able to cope with the undesirable effects anticipated from their progress.

But not all problems can be handled within the innovating organization, and even those that can are often susceptible to only partial solution. Take the problem of industrial retraining, for example. A large organization can forecast the new qualifications for workers and the shifts in the labor force that will accompany an innovation, and, having forecast them, can arrange the changes so as to minimize the cost and prepare the personnel to adjust to them. But it cannot control the more general effect of the innovation on the labor market, on the hierarchy of worker qualification, or on the social and spatial equilibrium of local communities; nor can it overcome resistance and opposition arising from people's attachment to customary relationships and to protective rules of social action which they have assimilated through education and socialization.

The difficulty is still greater in the case of problems that can be resolved only by a complete transformation of whole sectors of society: the disappearance of agricultural activities; the transformation of crafts, industries, regions; population migrations; development of mobility and risk; the breakdown of barriers protecting the ruling classes; et cetera. Obviously, economic organizations cannot be expected to assume responsibility for such matters. If one gave it to them, one would be investing them with powers that would threaten not only society but themselves. On the other hand, they would be paralyzed if they were obliged to adapt, willy-nilly, to a society that refused to change itself. Most frequently they are allowed to do as they please, after which the public authorities are asked to step in and cope with the worst of the material consequences of the changes—which is an utterly deplorable system. But to improve on this, society is going to have to develop new institutions that can anticipate and actively respond to these major problems.

It is, of course, the job of the state, and of the public authorities in general, to deal with such issues. But the extent of government intervention, and the rationalization for it, demands a new style of action, one completely different from the regulatory and distributive style of intervention to which most modern states remain bound. It is not merely a question of ensuring order and imposing a minimum of justice and social redistribution, as was the case in the past. Nor is it any longer a question of controlling economic circumstances, as we are now increasingly able to do. It is a question of making the collective investments necessary to prevent and minimize foreseeable structural crises and to develop the capacity of human groups and organizations to handle the direct and indirect consequences of their progress. The indicative planning developed in France was a beginning, although its relative ineffectiveness is now becoming apparent. Its value is that it has raised a problem people are now attempting to resolve both in free-enterprise nations and in nations inclined to *dirigisme* or socialism.

What is involved here is the promotion of new regulatory activities that will enable the economic and social actors to cope with all the consequences of change while leaving them really free. At the same time, it is necessary to maintain and develop better ways of measuring the results of social action within an ever greater network of complex systems.

This then raises a third problem: that of extending economic rationality to new fields of activity.

Both traditional and new collective public functions comprise the first field here. But education, research, health, the social services, welfare, the promotion of social and cultural activities, et cetera, are just as much part of this when they are not provided by public authorities as when they are. These activities are now so costly, and so important, that they can no longer be sheltered from the spirit of rational inquiry that has contributed so much to the success of classical productive activities. We may expect, and we have already seen, fierce reactions to this lifting of the spell that had been cast over a new and immense area of social life which until now conformed to pre-industrial forms of reasoning.* Yet it is quite probable that it is here that we shall see the greatest number of revolutionary innovations in the not too distant future.

* Psychiatric services are not alone in clinging to principles of organization deriving from an *ancien régime* style of thinking: schools, hospitals, and various other social and cultural services still favor a traditional organizational model, in flagrant contradiction to the rational goals they claim to pursue.

The main motive force of this revolution is going to be the takeover of activities formerly dominated by moral principles, by a mode of thought characteristic of scientific management. On the other hand, a very predictable repercussion will be that the extending of the rational model will naturally transform the model itself in the fields where it originated, viz.:

1. Management practice will be reduced more and more to abstract intellectual operations, stripped of their original ideology, which was profit; it may be that these abstract operations will be increasingly formalized and extended to cover all types of collective activity under all circumstances.

2. Far greater attention will be paid to human variables, which we shall have learned to deal with far more rationally, through the management of activities where these variables constitute the substance of the performance, not merely the means to its accomplishment. Perhaps the most important of these activities will be to support not only scientific research but also men of ideas who are capable of taking the risks of creative thought in new domains. We have only recently acknowledged the need for this, having mainly concentrated our attention on research in the exact sciences. But the movement is now gathering momentum and ought to spread, for, after all, a society's capacity for innovation depends on the breadth and effectiveness of a large group, including not only scientific researchers but also those who teach, translate, transmit, develop, and criticize discoveries in the natural and human sciences.

The growing need for development in this field raises some extremely complex problems of government, for advanced societies support a haphazard variety of activities that cannot be directly subjected to economic evaluation but that at the same time cannot entirely escape it without prejudicing the economic system, to whose maintenance they are indispensable. Consequently, it is likely that this sector too will be a fertile field for experiment in new forms of human relations and systems of government.

The Problem of Values

I have said that creativity and nonconformity are going to be fundamental values in the new society, along with rationalist rigor and social responsibility. And the better our understanding is of the circumstances likely to foster the development of creativity, the more we will tolerate individual idiosyncrasies; conversely, the demand for general conformity will decline. This vision may seem banal and unduly optimistic to those who have let themselves be influenced by the current hysteria, who believe that the development of technology and rationality promises only stifling conformity. But that fear bears witness, as it often has in history, more to a generalized kind of anxiety aroused by change than to any reasoned reaction to a genuine threat. If there really is a moral crisis, a crisis of civilization, then we should look for it in the opposite direction.

Belief in the development of a more creative, less conformist society in no way implies a belief that harmony is around the corner. On the contrary, creativity and nonconformity are far from reassuring values. When they were respected as aristocratic values—available only to superior beings, and as exceptions to the rule, destined to ennoble humanity without troubling the daily routine, which was dominated by narrower, bourgeois values—creativity and nonconformity were hardly dangerous. But the moment society has to accept creativity and nonconformity in all forms of activity, and for an increasing number of people in an ever more rational context, they become far more troublesome.

Men generally find it very hard to cope with any precise and ineluctable evaluation of the activities to which they commit themselves most heavily. To be fully responsible for one's own success—the evidence of one's "creativity," and not of one's cunning or one's connections—one probably has to confront far more problems than if one accepts the conformity we usually complain about, not to mention that mixture of aggressiveness and recrimination that characterizes the role of unlucky subordinate which so many of us seem content to play.

For all these reasons, increasingly powerful tensions are likely to develop in post-industrial societies. The present moral crisis is merely a foretaste, and we are entitled to ask whether the wave of hedonistic values now submerging the Western world is not simply the natural counterpart to the more vital, more creative, but also harder kind of civilization we are building.

CHAPTER THREE

Computerized Management

No innovation seems to have had a greater impact on the public imagination in recent years than the use of computers in business and public administration. Computers are a symbol of the future. They occupy a central place in all the futurist dreams of tomorrow's world. And the future they herald is already with us, since everyone is already jockeying for the best positions in the race for modernity. Even more important, computers are directly involved in communication, which is perhaps the central problem in human relations. Their advent threatens to add an entirely new dimension to our social life. Our experience of the problems facing society as a consequence of this new technology, so revolutionary in its modes of reasoning and in its possible consequences, is thus important to our subject.

It seems to me that our experience with computers well demonstrates the crying inadequacy of the narrowly technical analyses to which we have limited ourselves, and the inadequacy of purely instrumental analyses of technological development. It also demonstrates how essential it is to think in terms of human relationships and the power structure, as well as in terms of technical rationality, if we are to understand and successfully negotiate the process of change.

The computers' extraordinary capacities for data-collection, for memorization, and for logical and arithmetical reasoning make them by far the best management tools man has ever possessed, but their success, which is intended to further the rationalization of whatever enterprise they have been put in, ultimately depends on the human groups employing them developing a greater capacity for cooperation among themselves. Concentrating on a purely technical, utilitarian approach, without taking human problems into account (apart from those concerning intellectual training), is likely not only to arouse needless fears and blind resistance but to result in failure in the most practical and financial sense of the word.

The problem is, of course, not new. Engineers and humanists have clashed before. Major technological changes were successful in the past only when men, instead of adapting to some rational model devised by engineers, developed a new system of human relationships enabling them to benefit from the opportunities presented by the new technology and to control its development. But the evolutionary time cycle of the relationship between man and technology was so long that the relationship remained obscure. The growth of new orders and collective capacities was slow, a process of trial and error, of myopic actions and reactions. This can no longer be so where computers are concerned—for all the reasons examined in the preceding chapter, but also because computers intervene directly in human relations, since they deal not with matter but with the essentially human phenomenon of communication. The introduction of computers is therefore exemplary, since to some extent it prefigures the mode of change, and the mode of thinking about change, that will characterize the world of tomorrow.

Is Information Neutral?

When experts draw up an integrated information system for a business, they start from the premise that information is completely neutral, that is to say, that it can be exchanged at all levels and between all persons at no cost other than time.

But in business, as in any organization or system of human relationships, information is not neutral. Information is power, and sometimes, for a brief moment, it is the essential instrument of power. No one communicates information without at least intuitively taking into account the possible consequences to his power position. The withholding of information is not only an affective phenomenon, it is a rational means of government (or countergovernment).

People communicate not because they are capable of communicating or because they dispose of effective instruments of communication. They communicate because they want to, and they want to because it is useful to them to do so. This explains why, in the same organization, certain pieces of information never get through although they are repeated constantly, while others overcome apparently insuperable barriers.

The obstacles to applying the computer specialist's theoretically rational system in a real social system such as a business are therefore far greater than is generally realized. It is not just that habits have to be changed, or that interests are threatened by the new techniques (after all, if we understood them, we could effectively manipulate them or even buy them off). What is involved is a whole body of practices and arrangements which in effect are the real government of the enterprise or, if one prefers, the implicit rules governing the relations between men, groups, and categories.

Let us take an example—somewhat extreme but actually true. A large firm commissions some computer specialists to draw up a system that makes it possible to control production on the basis of demand from a limited but highly variable clientele. The problem is vitally important to the business, since its production problems can only be resolved either by adopting a policy entailing a dangerous increase in costs or with a policy entailing the loss (albeit temporary) of numerous customers.

This is a technically difficult but not intractable problem. The computer specialists produce a system that is tried out for a time in the smallest production unit in the firm, and it appears to work satisfactorily. But when it is introduced into the main production unit, it is a complete failure and has to be abandoned entirely—all because of a problem no one had foreseen.

The information concerning the amount of time it takes to manufacture one item, information which is necessary in regulating the plant's production, is also used to calculate the workers' pay. This information, however, is systematically falsified as a result of a tacit agreement between local management, the foremen, and the employees. Officially, the factory applies the regionally agreed branch rate, but it is able to pay more, and the workers are strong enough to demand more. So the easiest way around this has been to cheat on the time records. Now the obvious question is why, if all participants agree, do they not simply recognize the facts openly and adjust the norms so that they correspond to the work actually being done and to the actual rate of wages? This would be the obvious solution, but in this factory it is out of the question, because the parties involved would prefer to make the arrangements secretly rather than recognize the true nature of their relationship. This is so because they thereby retain a margin for negotiation, as well as the potentiality for any number of more or less secret subordinate arrangements—all of which is very useful in oiling the wheels of the whole endeavor.

Admittedly, such a situation will only rarely occur in precisely these terms, but similar mechanisms constantly affect the relationships between the various factors and functions involved in the management of small as well as large units.

Standardizing the information needed to achieve the requisite precision and rigor brings to light some of the results of each party's activities, but it also brings into question its sources of power. When people start fighting to maintain their own department's or division's filing system, they are fighting not merely over questions of routine but for their power. On another level, they are fighting to preserve their capacity to do their job well, since this depends on a margin of freedom provided by the exclusive, or anticipated, possession of certain information.

Are we then to conclude that integrated systems are unworkable? Of course not. One cannot abandon the attempt to change just because change poses some problems. But we must assess the obstacles carefully, and above all we must define our objectives more modestly and from a more developmental point of view. The best system is not the most rational one but the one that enables a business or an organization to evolve most rapidly.

It is all too easy to fulminate against deplorable practices favored in this or that company. These practices, it should be remembered, are a means of government—and better a bad means of government than no government at all. Most businesses, in fact, are still far from being rational organizations. A business consists of a whole range of fiefs, of networks of complicity, of little secrets and private arrangements. Mostly, it is a matter of arranging for mutual protection, and the general management only very superficially disturbs this game, by means of interventions that are themselves a good deal less rational than one might think.

Businesses do, of course, evolve. In France the discovery of modern management methods will probably lead to a more general mutation toward a more rational organizational model. Computers give us the means; but we should beware of thinking that change is the automatic outcome of the introduction of computers.

The Changing Business Organization

To gain a more comprehensive, more concrete view of this change, we must examine the three main hierarchic levels of any business, since the computer revolution has a very different effect in each case.

For a long time it was believed that most problems raised by the introduction of computers occurred at the level of production. We still tend to project our myths about robots enslaved by machines on this level. Yet experience has shown that the advent of computers poses fewer problems here than at any other level.

The reason for this is simple. Electronic machines did not bring about standardization here, because it existed already. They did not rob workers of their prerogatives, for these had already been lost. If the reaction was docile and apathetic, it was because workers had lost the habit of involving themselves in their own working lives. It was as if the employees had signed a tacit psychological contract permitting them to say to management, "You have turned us into operatives; we obey you without trying to understand the reasons for your decisions. In exchange, we demand to stay free, that is, not to become psychologically involved in how the business runs."

This explains the workers' lack of resistance to computers and the lack of interest in information about them. And it explains why subordinates accept change while refusing to become concerned about it. Paradoxically, a successful information campaign is more likely to arouse criticism and general discontent among employees than complete silence. But the discontent is not necessarily a bad sign. On the contrary, the breakdown of the psychological docility and apathy lets the employees benefit more fully from the opportunities for higher qualifications and promotion made available by the introduction of new machinery; at the same time, it enables the business to mobilize fresh resources among its personnel. But management usually tends to get cold feet at this stage and, faced with mounting pressure, prefers to break off all contact.

To go further, management should be ready to face the problems raised by supervisory personnel. This is the truly sensitive point, both for the classic operations of administrative automation (accounts, payroll, statistics) which directly affect most of the subordinate employees, and for those operations more or less directly affecting management.

And it is at this supervisory level that the advent of computers is likely to have a positively revolutionary impact. The lower grades are forced into the ranks of operatives—in fact, the lowest of these had precious little influence already. The people who are really hit are the ones with positions of specific responsibility: department or division heads, agency managers, and field officers. Up until now these people acted as communication relays, and they had a great deal of influence. Their influence grew as administration became more complex and as they mastered procedural detail and ways around it. Since it was impossible to do without them, they enjoyed prestige, importance, and sometimes a wage not always justified by their competence. But the computer revolution made the routine experience of all these middle-grade executives obsolete. Developing a strategy of mobility and cooperation to take the place of defensive and self-protective strategies is particularly important at their level. Management tends instinctively to rely upon the loyalty and faithfulness of executives at this level, but it is precisely these qualities which inspire the protective stratagems so detrimental to the business.

The problem changes in nature when we introduce a more integrated system of management, for here management personnel itself is directly threatened. Difficulties are usually attributed to resistance among the supervisory grades—and it is true that they can hardly help resisting—but the key to success must be sought at a still higher level. An integrated system can work successfully only if management undergoes a complete transformation. Management must abandon its administrative role in favor of a policy role; this implies a very different type of specialization, as well as the development of new human relations among members of the "team."

This mutation in the role of management should lead to a change in the business's mode of government. Of course, computers introduce indispensable techniques, but the issue is still essentially an organizational one, at least if we give this term a very broad meaning, including human behavior as well as structure. Change here will consist in decentralization, delegation of responsibility, the setting up of autonomous decision-making centers free to run themselves but sanctioned in accordance with the results obtained (which we are only now learning how to measure). Large American corporations introduced these methods long before they introduced computers, and this has been one reason for their more rapid and successful development in computerized management.

As we are now beginning to realize, it is only when general management divests itself of the petty tasks of day-to-day administration that it becomes possible to rationalize administration. Obstinate retention of these functions is one of the biggest obstacles there is to successful computer-based management.

Computers and Society

Computers do not, unfortunately, make social change happen, but their use gives so many advantages to those capable of innovating in organizational arrangements that their coming brings revolutionary ferment. What this means in the end is that the capacity to innovate socially and institutionally is more important than technical prowess.

Even very modern societies change only with great difficulty. And there are huge differences among societies where structure, traditions, and the resulting styles of action are concerned. But the new industrial revolution demands that we overcome these difficulties. Let us, by way of conclusion, take a look at what I consider are the three main ones: the problem of open communication; the problem of freedom and individual risk; and the problem of institutional change.

The computer revolution can be carried out successfully only if individuals, groups, and society as a whole accept first, and very generally, more open and more transparent relationships, and if they consciously accept the consequences of their decisions and their behavior.

In the case of France, the social system is stuck fast in a system of partitions and barriers, of secrecy and irresponsibility, so that difficult decisions are fudged and each individual is assured the system's general protection from all sanctions— even that of publicity. Groups, categories, and even individuals refuse to confront one another directly. The protective shadow of secrecy, complexity, and state intervention is needed to solve a problem or sweep it under the carpet. If this model continues much longer, French society will miss out on the computer revolution. The crisis of May 1968 revealed a deep uneasiness about this subject, but it came nowhere near producing a constructive solution.

The second problem is that of freedom and individual risk. There is a tendency to believe that the greatest danger of our age lies in the menace of standardization. But, on the contrary, the computer revolution in fact requires a greater capacity for individual freedom and autonomy. Yet most executives, perhaps most citizens, object to computers and to this potential for freedom. They reject them because they are risky, and because they prefer the security of a stalemate society.

The new and currently popular myth of teamwork can be and is used as a new line of defense by traditional protectionists. In the name of team spirit, differences are papered over, responsibilities are diffused, and traditional feudal solidarities are strengthened. In fact, the most effective organizations are those in which the individual is considered just as important as the team, those in which a man is expected to be able to stand up to his colleagues as well as cooperate with them, those whose teams are easily formed, broken up, or re-formed.

The third, perhaps more immediately important problem, where our transformed thinking may be more rapidly influential, concerns the strategy of change. Computers are a manifestation of modern society's entry into an era of permanent change. In these circumstances, contrary to what is popularly supposed, the proportion of what is known to what is not known is actually decreasing, and we can no longer work with *a priori* models that we imagine are definitive (if only temporarily).

All this suggests that it is much less important to think about objectives than it is to think about institutions. We should avoid fixing objectives that will have become obsolete before they can be attained. Instead, we must establish institutions capable of fostering constant innovation, correcting their objectives as we receive fresh data and obtain new results.

"Institutional capacity"—the capacity to foster, create, and re-create living institutions (institutions capable of transforming themselves)—would thus seem to be the final key to change. We are concerned here not only with the governmental aspects of this capacity, for a business's success depends upon it just as much. It is essential that in either field we evolve a new conception of the leader's role and activities. Leaders must cease to be managers and become guides, inspirers, and midwives to new social systems. They should be concerned far more with the real development of the human groups they direct than with applying rational models devised by engineers and technicians.

The computer revolution is not going to impose a rational model on any human enterprise, since no rational model exists as such; but it will enable the enterprise to become more rational—that is, if the people belonging to it learn to behave more rationally among themselves. They stand a better chance of doing so if *a priori* models are not imposed on them.

CHAPTER FOUR

The Problem of Participation

The idea of participation has become a myth common to all Western societies. The need to transform power relations, the need for simpler and more effective human relationships and forms of cooperation—both are expected to be filled by this latest of panaceas.

In France, General de Gaulle's decision in 1968 to gamble what remained of his moral authority on this confused and already rather moth-eaten ideology could only end in failure. Nor has anyone anywhere else been able to find a simple solution in participatory arrangements. Nonetheless, the problem of participation remains a key one in post-industrial society, in some respects the reverse side of all the problems of power, innovation, and development we have just examined.

French society can move ahead only if it moves away from the model of government which is the consequence of the passion for command, control, and simplistic logic animating its senior officials, businessmen, technicians, and governing mandarins. All of them are too clever, too competent, and, equally, too overwhelmed by the nation's demands for economic and social development, against which they blindly try to preserve their caste barriers.

What was attractive to the French about the myth of participation was that it restated—less disquietingly and, it was hoped, more realistically—the moral condemnation of this kind of government that was formulated in the course of the revolt of May 1968. The moralism was insipid and the realism miserably narrow-minded, but behind the dream, as behind the myth of salvation-through-revolution that re-emerged in May 1968, it was clear that the real issue being confronted was that of the role of the individual in an increasingly complex, ever more changing and demanding society.

Three Illusions

No country can be cured of its illness by offering its citizens some mystical participation in the essence of power. Their social ills will gradually disappear when they finally get around to transforming their institutions and modes of action so that they can reasonably look after their own affairs, take their own risks, and make the mistakes they have to make in order to progress. In other words, participation is too important to be left to ideologues and politicians. And if progress is to be made, we must first dispel the myths surrounding this topic.

The first of these myths is that there was a pre-industrial golden age. What we actually find in this romantic dream, which is entertained by many of our contemporaries, is a nostalgic longing for a more fraternal, "primitive" community in which, it is believed, a human being could enjoy a more balanced, more human life. The modern world has grown too complex, competitive, violent; if it has not transformed man into a machine, it has at any rate made him too rational. Participation, then, would enable us to rediscover our lost roots, the richness and humanity of which the bustling consumer society has robbed us. The events of May 1968 in France revived this generous but naïve anarchist tendency.

This is not a left-wing tendency, any more than it is reactionary. Left-wing radical students, Marshall McLuhan, psycho-sociologists advocating group therapy, and various generations of corporatists meet on common ground here, and all partake in the myth of tribal brotherhood.

The idyllic vision of a golden age long past—or yet to come—founded on the small group has no foundation in fact. Obviously the inhabitants of a village are closer to one another than the residents of a municipal housing development, and they certainly take part in running their community. But what kind of decisions do they make, and what initiatives are open to them? They decide according to custom, and their initiatives are sharply limited by the pressures of their fellow citizens. Their participation is instinctive, if not unconscious; it implies an absence of differentiation in the group and is accompanied by heavy constraints upon the individual.

If we go back as far as the primitive tribal community, we can see that each member certainly does participate, but he is suffocated by his participation to the point where any notion of personal existence is impossible. If he were cut off from his community, he would be disabled and would have great difficulty in surviving. The decision-making methods of certain African communities might be taken to represent an ideal form of total participation: decisions are preceded by long palavers, in the course of which each member adds his voice to the chorus, until finally everyone sings in unison. But what revolutionary would accept the extraordinary limitations which inevitably accompany this sort of collective commitment, and which treats deviants as traitors, to be expelled from the human community?

In truth, the nostalgia for community life expresses the fears that are naturally aroused when we face the psychological difficulties of making choices and confronting our fellow men, the anxiety we have when faced with freedom and risk. The small community is a mythical refuge. We must take seriously the malaise to which its popularity bears witness, but it has never been of interest as a cure or even as a realistic contribution to the debate.

A second illusion surrounding the idea of participation

concerns affective participation: the idea that men participate insofar as we are able to arouse their affectivity. They need to devote themselves to something, to outdo themselves, to become enthusiastic. One must "win their hearts." In this rationalized, disembodied modern world, the argument goes, we badly need to restore the affectivity from which we have been cut off. The really effective leader is the one who finds words to move his fellow men, with whom others can identify, who strikes a chord in men's souls.

No one can deny that citizens or members of any organization need to commit themselves and surpass themselves, but the dangers arising from an overhasty interpretation of this can be frightening. After all, enthusiasm for a cause and identification with a leader have always been used as levers with which to manipulate the masses. A number of sociological studies have demonstrated that the ideal conditions for affective participation are realized in times of war, and it is only reasonable to ask whether we should really seek to build a society upon this kind of participation.*

Affective participation ought, rather, to be seen as a sort of alienation that imprisons both those who submit to it and those who use it for their own ends. It is a coarse, rigid, and inefficient kind of collective bond, and any evolution in this direction is a step backward. It needs to be said once again, clearly and firmly, that in the modern world there can be no acceptable participation that is not founded on a conscious and rational model—conscious, because only insofar as we are conscious will participation have a truly human dimension; rational, because only in the rational world can we hope to escape manipulation. Of course we need to be together and to involve ourselves emotionally in our common life, but why should we hand over responsibility for it to powers beyond us? When participation in the affairs of the community is properly and consciously balanced in rational relationships, it will not be less affective for

* So as not to offend, I am deliberately avoiding any mention of fascism, Maoism, or Castroism.

that. Our demands for affectivity here are as distorted as the psychoanalytic patient's refusal to accept the reality principle.

Consciousness and rationality are not enough, however, to dispel the myth of participation. There is still another illusion, deeply rooted in the collective consciousness. It consists in the belief in business and managerial circles that participation is a gift bestowed by leaders on their subordinates, and, among workers, that the right to participation is a natural right that must be seized from those who wield power. Opposed as these two views may be, they stem from the same philosophy, and their application has always led to the same failures.

The industrialist who bestows upon his employees the right to participate in decision-making invariably reaps ingratitude from the very people to whom he thought he was being so generous. The employees will in general remain apathetic or will use the rights conceded to them only to thwart his authority. Unions, on the other hand, find that the co-management process invites skepticism and trouble with the rank and file, who would rather criticize than assume responsibility. Only affective manipulation enables both sides to maintain an acceptable climate and turn failure into semi-success.

Why should this be so? Quite simply, participation can be neither a gift nor an advantage. It is a burden, sometimes a heavy one. When it is offered to subordinates, it is natural that they should be only mildly enthusiastic about it, propaganda notwithstanding—a response that has been observed in a number of sociological studies, in France and elsewhere, but that still comes as a surprise. Yet what could be more natural? To participate is to lose some of one's freedom; it means abandoning the normally comfortable, sheltered position of the critic; it means running the risks of emotional commitment; it means submitting to the constraints of someone else, to the group or unit in whose decision-making process one participates. At a deeper level, each member of an organization has his own habits, his own skills and personal practices, and these are so many secrets enabling him to do his job at the least cost to himself—so much capital, as it were, ensuring him a certain minimum freedom of maneuver. And it is this which he would be asked to commit to the process of participation. Who would agree to do so unless he hoped to gain something as a result? Who would risk his capital without any serious guarantee or chance of getting a return on it?

For a subordinate, participation makes sense only if it is paid for in terms of money, power, or prospects for the future, since it is going to cost those involved both affectively and rationally. If it is thought that the participation of subordinates is worth this kind of investment, in terms of increased advantages accruing to the organization attempting it, then a price must be paid commensurate with the potential gains. But if, on the other hand, it is thought that subordinates have little to offer and that the only reason to let them participate is to please them, or because it is fashionable, or because it might raise morale, then it is not worth trying, and failure is a foregone conclusion.

The Conditions for Conscious and Rational Participation

Conscious and rational participation, based on the idea of free negotiation, and viewed neither as a paternalistic gift nor as a political struggle, requires conditions quite different from the legal conditions obtaining, for example, in France.

The first of these conditions seems to me to be the radical transformation of our idea of rational action. In most of the modern world, both public life and industry act according to an idea of rationality directly inspired by Taylor's principle: "Once a goal has been fixed, there is always one best way of arriving at it." This principle certainly had merits, for it made it possible to substitute the engineer's rational decisions for the intuitive directives of traditional potentates. But we can now go further than this, and the idea of participation requires that we do so.

If there is only one best way to attain a given objective, there is surely no need, once the goal has been fixed, to discuss the issue and ask everyone his opinion about it. All that has to be done is to get a competent technician to find the best way (or ways). The reader may argue that means are secondary and can be left to the engineers; what is important is to discuss the objectives themselves. But if this were so, there would be no hope, and 99 per cent of the human race would be condemned never to exert the slightest influence over the activities which shape their lives. This is because nearly all of us live in a world of "means"—all the elements of which could easily be determined by technicalities, if technicalities were effectively governed by the "one best way" principle.

But, as we know well, there is always some discussion concerning means, and engineers normally have to introduce "tolerances" that permit adjustments to be made. Still, obedience to the principle of rationality makes discussion very difficult. Engineers are reluctant to accept any questions about what should be considered within the realm of pure technique (as, for example, in job evaluation: tools, work-rates, environment). Bad faith on one hand and suspicion on the other are instinctive forms of behavior making rational participation impossible.

To believe that open discussions about objectives can remedy these difficulties is to believe in the virtues of manipulation or in those of the spontaneous creativity of the masses. They are equally uncertain and very closely related.

The current evolution toward ever greater rationalization in the choice of objectives runs exactly counter to these illusions. If effective and meaningful participation develops, it must occur at levels considered to come within the sphere of means. In a business, this indicates that the definition of how tasks will be executed becomes strategically important.

This is rationally possible because the "one best way" principle is merely a convenient simplification which has long since lost its utility. The more we understand the parameters defining a field of action, the less rigid we need be in our definitions of a problem, and the more readily we can see that means need not be separated from ends, and that the most rational approach is one which compares ends/means sets with each other.

This is the core of all problems of participation. When—in a factory, for example—a worker's job is modified so that in the new arrangement he is isolated from his former workmates, all that has been made, apparently, is a slight technical change. In reality, however, it is quite possible that the whole climate on the factory floor has been upset, and that production from the workers now laboring in isolation will decline, even if the new division of labor was theoretically more rational. This may lead management to investigate the reasons for the change and to modify its entire policy in this sector of the plant, in order to reconcile the employees' desire for collective work with the desired goal. This is what I mean by an ends/means set.

In this perspective, which has been opened up for us by recent advances in decision-making theory, one of the most serious obstacles to developing participation is the type of training our engineers now receive: a narrow, deductive model of rationality which (especially in France) we are unable to shake off.

Another obstacle comes from our conception of organizational logic. If we consider that efficiency can be obtained only in using rigid, machine-like armies, participation will remain a dream. But this is not the case. Organizational techniques have made great progress: the more we understand human behavior and the parameters of a given action, the more we are able to abandon forms of management based on constraint in favor of those founded on forecasting.

Any organization needs a certain minimum of conformity from its members, for it could not otherwise coordinate their work or integrate them into the complex models essential to productive, commercial, or research undertakings. But this need for conformity is great only because our understanding of human behavior is poor. Early large organizations used ideological or physical constraints to achieve conformity, turning their members into veritable automata. (It is not in our electronic world but in the eighteenth century that we find "robot-men.") In our own time, if participation is to become possible and effective, organizations will have to abandon rigid, bureaucratic, constraining models in favor of a more flexible and tolerant model based on mobility, competition, and negotiation. Our task, then, is not to contain overpowerful organizations, but to persuade them to modernize themselves in the full sense of the term.

The development of this new model depends above all on the development of individuals themselves. Participation is possible only when modern man becomes more demanding, freer, and better able to bear the tensions of collective responsibility.

A number of surveys carried out in private and state-owned organizations have shown us that the employees most capable of participating, the ones who were best informed and most interested in a firm's activities, were not the good, loyal, and faithful employees in the traditional sense, but those who seemed to be least bound to the organization. The traditional business policy of binding employees to the company makes no sense, therefore, where participation is concerned, for the stability obtained is bought at the price of wastage in human resources. This paradox may be shocking to some people, but it conforms to the simplest psychological analysis. One can commit oneself effectively only if one is free. The traditional organization man, imprisoned within his allegiances and loyalties, cannot run the risks entailed in participation. If he has committed his entire life to the company, he cannot compromise it by expressing unorthodox opinions. So he practices self-restraint and tries to protect himself; eventually these limitations and protections have their effect on the life of the company as a whole, tending to paralyze it.

At the same time, the freedom essential to participation demands a very large measure of adaptability. One wonders whether this tradition of passive loyalty, together with a passion for security (which plays a great role among lower executives and middle-management workers in France, for example), may not constitute one of the basic difficulties in the development of participation.

The Long-Term Trends

Modern society offers many opportunities for development, and the facile pessimism which it pleases so many intellectuals to adopt cannot possibly be supported by any honest comparative analysis. Although society's claims on parts of our life are increasing, signifying a growing number of constraints, modern man is becoming freer and better able to make conscious commitments. Of course, this new liberty is no longer a safeguard against one's fellow man but indicates, rather, a capacity to change and act within a more and more complex social structure. But the individual is now better able to make choices, both in cultural or political matters and in his everyday material existence. We are less and less limited by our social condition, and the most humble and least privileged among us now enjoy a freedom of choice that was never available before.

So the struggle for participation should emphatically not be directed *against* the development of post-industrial society, but should base itself on the possibilities it offers. The pessimism of those who foresee an excessively restrictive society in the future and who want to halt current evolution is not only ill-founded but positively harmful. Neither concentration nor complexity is a danger. What is dangerous is the continued anxious desire for protection in a society which in fact requires that we heighten individual freedom.

As for the risks of being manipulated, they stem from those traditional illusions about community life or affective participation. We tend to compare the constraints we live under with those to which our fathers were subjected, without taking into account the human capacity to adjust and countermanipulate over the course of time. As constraints have multiplied, man has developed means to circumvent them and safeguard his freedom. We ought to have faith in man's powers of invention and, in fighting to increase his freedom, should not be afraid of advancing toward a more complex society.

If the evolution of societies in general inclines us toward a reasonable optimism, the situation in France nevertheless presents a number of very profound problems that account for the gravity of the crisis she is currently passing through. It is no accident that the myth of participation should have gained such a strong hold over the French. The more the French repeat the word, the more they reject, if not the thing, at least the conditions indispensable to its development.

The weight of bureaucratic centralization, the effect of a long tradition of military command, and the development of industries that have taken the government or the army as their organizational model, have accustomed the French to a general pattern of centralization that is tempered only by an anarchic system of privileges and by worthy paternalistic sentiments. This kind of system naturally creates a gulf between managers and executants, rigid relationships between human groups, constricting interplay founded on defensiveness and self-protection, and a general desire for security on the part of everyone. Even within a given enterprise, relations between individuals at different levels are strained, as a consequence of which each person is thrown back upon his peer group, which alone is capable of providing him with the necessary protection. As a result, we have in France a stratified situation in which each group fights to protect its privileges. The consequences of this are apparent in the very functioning of business, where the most serious obstacle to participation is found in pressure exerted by the group on the individual in order to maintain group cohesion. Cultural constraints, nevertheless, leave a fair amount of freedom of action, and if organizations cannot overcome all barriers, they can at least mobilize the resources available in the existing system.

The basic principle of all participation is not communication (information) or dialogue (whether about major objectives or minor means), but negotiation (hence confrontation, which gives rise to compromise) about the most practical elements of everyday life. (This negotiation is not to be confused with labor-management negotiations, which are usually concerned with the protection and security of wages and employment.) It will be difficult to achieve, for it poses a threat to the entire stability and daily management of business, but it is well worth running the risk.

PART TWO
FRENCH SOCIETY: STALEMATE SOCIETY

French society is profoundly conservative in its modes of organization and its models of human relations. It is also anarchic, with a taste for revolt and a long tradition of utopian protest.

The contradiction is not, in fact, so intolerable as it may seem at first sight, for the two attitudes are closely complementary. All societies hold contradictory and complementary oppositions within them, and the cultural crisis of the past few years has revealed similar paradoxes in other societies, particularly in the United States. In France, however, the paradox has found articulate expression over a much longer period of time; one might even say it has become institutionalized. And in this contradiction and complementarity the hidden mainsprings of the French political and social process are to be found. In any case, the opposing vicious circles of protest and stagnation, mutually generating and reinforcing each other, are more immediately perceptible and are easier to analyze.

To throw them into relief, we shall study each of them in turn: the French administrative model in the specific example of public bureaucracy and the style of action it fosters; and French revolutionary ferment in the example of the crisis in the French universities and the social and political crisis of May and June 1968.

CHAPTER FIVE

The French Bureaucratic Style

The archetype of France's mode of government and, more generally, its characteristic style of action, is the administrative model of management and control.

This mode of government appears to be in a state of crisis, as the style of action it has engendered throughout French society becomes less and less appropriate to the problems that society and its many subsystems must now resolve. Yet it has considerable powers of resistance, and no new style of action has emerged to take its place.

The Permanence of the French Administrative Style

French public administration, like all vast human institutions, is a disparate ensemble of bits and pieces, and the demarcations among the different elements are never very precise. It is, moreover, a living, hence constantly evolving, ensemble, and it is hard to define its conditions at any one moment. Yet behind its apparent diversity and complexity, its evolution and change, any analysis with claims to thoroughness will uncover a few extremely stable characteristics.

Since the publication of Tocqueville's *The Ancien Régime and the Revolution*, four regimes have followed one upon the other,

77

the number of public officials has grown tenfold, the administration's tasks have multiplied and been transformed; the use of the telephone, typewriter, and now electronics has transfigured human relations among civil servants and the conditions of administrative action. Yet Tocqueville's vigorous tirade against that "regulating and constricting administration, attempting to foresee everything, taking care of everything, always better aware of the citizen's interests than is the citizen himself, ever active, and sterile," * seems just as fresh and relevant today as when he wrote it. Some of his remarks might very well serve today as an introductory report for a discussion group of young reformist civil servants. It is not uncommon, moreover, to find a copy of excerpts from *La Dime Royale*† prominently placed on the desk of some provincial public-works contractor, made available to him by his professional association. And if you ask the master of the establishment the purpose of this publication, the violence of his attack on the system whereby contracts are awarded will convince you that Vauban's indignation has the same affective impact today as it had on contractors at the time of Louis XIV. Two and a half centuries later, despite revolutions, wars, and the advent of the machine age, positions do not seem to have shifted an inch.

We must conclude, then, that there are certain constants in behavior, or rather in human relationships, specific to the functioning of the French administrative machine. These have survived the test of time, as well as the transformation of techniques, beliefs, customs, and at least the ostensible goals of society. I have attributed the preservation of these constants to the existence of a system of extremely stable homeostatic relations, which I have termed the French bureaucratic model.‡

Let us summarize briefly the essential characteristics of this system. Obviously, it is a very centralized system. But the principal feature of its centralization, as all observers have

---

* A. de Tocqueville, *L'Ancien Régime et la Révolution* (Paris, 1953), I, 287.
† A famous pamphlet written in 1707 by Marshal Vauban.
‡ See Michel Crozier, *The Bureaucratic Phenomenon* (Chicago, 1964), p. 294.

recognized, is not that it concentrates absolute power at the top of the pyramid, but that it places a sufficient distance, or protective screen, between those competent to make decisions and those affected by them. The power that concentrates at the top of the pyramid is mostly formal power, restricted by an absence of information and living contacts. The decision-makers lack the means to grasp the practical aspects of the problems they have to deal with, while those who have the knowledge lack the power to make decisions. The gulf between the two groups, or rather between the two roles, recurs with almost fatal regularity. It makes for an excellent protective barrier for the superiors, who are unlikely to suffer the consequences of their decisions, as well as for the subordinates, who are free from the fear of intrusion into their problems from above.

This tradition of centralization is related to another characteristic, less frequently recognized but just as fundamental: stratification. French public authorities are highly stratified along functional and, above all, along hierarchic lines. It is hard to move from one category to another, and communication between categories is poor. The rule of equality determines relationships within each category, and group pressure on the individual is considerable.

This system does offer certain advantages—stability, regularity, and predictability. But at the same time it is extremely rigid, and it naturally generates routine. Since subordinates benefit from withholding information, superiors cannot obtain practical knowledge of the variables that should be taken into account; consequently they tend either to rely on abstract regulations or to take refuge in precedents. Centralization and stratification are such insuperable barriers to communication that the consequences of "bureaucratic" decisions take a long time to become apparent. The system cannot learn from its mistakes, and it has a constant tendency to close in upon itself.

To cope with the difficulties posed in this mode of organization, those at the top must try to foresee and settle everything in advance. This is clearly impossible, and so the system is forced to tolerate a great many exceptions, arising and clustering

around zones of uncertainty that can never be wholly elimi-
nated. The officials whose job it is to deal with these situations
seize the opportunity thus presented to assert their power within
the system, and against it. This is what leads to the formation
and preservation of feudalities and privileges, which both those
at the top of the system and the rank and file find utterly
unacceptable. And it is, I suspect, the specific and rational
source for the violent passion aroused in the French civil
servant when he is confronted with privilege and favoritism,
constantly driving the system toward greater centralization.
Much of his time is spent fighting the consequences of the
administration's lack of adaptation to reality, a situation which
his very struggle merely serves to exacerbate.

Since local adjustments are considered as no more than
temporary palliatives—a stretching of the rules dictated by
circumstances—and not as experiments or attempts at reform
that might contribute to progress, change occurs only when the
sum of mistakes and inadaptations becomes so great that, even
if it does not threaten the survival of the entire system, it at least
endangers its stability. Change then takes the form of a crisis
that disturbs the system while preserving its principles and its
rigidity.

Some Examples of Typical Blockages

My analysis here is not founded upon a deductive model but
has been developed out of specific case studies and can be
applied to all kinds of different administrative practices of
which we have personal experience. In these practices we can
see that the French administrative style is ultimately a decision-
making method, based on bad or faulty communication which
spares susceptibilities on all levels of (or among partners in) an
administrative operation, at the expense of efficiency and
outcome.

We are now going to take a brief look at four very different
examples of this, which I think will demonstrate the persistence

of the same mechanism in situations and processes that are
entirely unique and different.

We can begin with the buffer-grade, or umbrella process. Let
us take the case of a large, highly mechanized, administrative
organization whose task is to carry out repetitive accounting
operations. This organization gives the public good service, but
it functions badly, being very taxing to its personnel without at
the same time being satisfactorily productive. Morale is low,
even at the executive grades, but the leadership at the managerial or ministerial level minimizes this problem, attributing it to
general phenomena that no one can do anything about, such as
technological change.

A survey of the personnel enabled us to demonstrate that, on
the contrary, the poor functioning and low morale were due to
the buffer-grade process. The most sensitive point in the
organization concerns the majority of employees, who work as
accounting-machine operators. Contrary to what is believed at
the highest levels, these employees enjoy good relations with
their immediate supervisors but complain violently about their
senior supervisors, with whom they have practically no contact
at all. The mechanism accounting for this paradox is simple and
wholly logical. The senior executives decide in detail on all
matters directly affecting the daily working lives of the employees—notably possible modifications of the workload and grant-
ing time off. When making these decisions they have to rely
entirely on information supplied by their subordinates. But the
latter have an interest in deceiving their superiors, since they are
all competing among themselves to obtain, within an organization dominated by scarcity, the means necessary to ensure the
proper functioning of their units; they thus have to falsify the
information they supply, if they are to influence the decisions in
their favor.* Knowing that they are being misinformed, senior
executives generally opt for the least-risk approach: that is, they
rely on impersonal, routine decisions, which are inadequate

* They have nothing to gain from cultivating the favor of their superiors, since the
latter are unable to reward them, promotion being based on seniority.

both to the individuals concerned and from the point of view of organizational efficiency.

The reaction of each player conforms to the expectations aroused in a perfectly internalized scenario. A group that is deprived of extra help or an employee who is refused a leave of absence blames the mean, or badly informed, senior executive; the subordinate supervisor protests loudly that he was not listened to; the senior executive takes refuge in the silence of regulations, knowing full well that the incidents will recur, canceling each other out, and that he would face still greater problems if, in an attempt to improve the quality of his decisions, he tried to break through the impermeable screen formed by the buffer grade—the subordinate supervisors.

How does a system that is utterly absurd from these various points of view manage to continue to function? It does so because everyone is, at one and the same time, its victim and its accomplice. Employees are spared the dangers of direct dependence on their chief, and they feel protected by the buffer grade. Subordinate supervisors are protected both from the employees, for whom they are not finally responsible, and from their superiors, who cannot interfere with their activities. And the senior executives do not have to take any risks and are not responsible, in fact, for anything. Everyone, finally, seems to prefer these blockages and bickerings to the risk of conflict and responsibility. The buffer grade—a well-concealed though very common form of umbrella practice—is a vital element in the institutionalized noncommunication that characterizes the internal functioning of French government.

Let us consider another situation. Petty bureaucrats and minor officials are generally thought of as docile executants of a meddlesome government policy, who take unjust revenge on the general public for their own problems. But in one situation most propitious for the development of this kind of behavior, our surveys have uncovered very different attitudes. Minor employees in prefectorial offices*—the kind of people the public has to

---

* There are ninety prefects in France, each one in charge of one *département,* the basic unit of French administrative life, something in between a county and a state.

deal with at the counter—were extremely critical of the government administration, and their comments were in complete agreement with those of the general public. As in the preceding case, their resentment was directed against a higher grade—management—which in this case meant the members of the prefectorial corps.

Here, however, the process was far more complex. The managerial grade derives its power from the fact that it alone has the authority to permit more flexible application of regulations. But if this freedom is to have any meaning, the rules must normally be observed to the letter. So the petty officials have to be mean and niggling if the prefect or director is to show up well. Thus manipulated by a system that turns them into despised instruments of a policy that completely betrays the spirit of the rules they are supposed to apply, the executants rebel both by attacking the system from the general public's viewpoint and by pressuring the higher grades to stop making exceptions. The only possible consequence of this pressure is to make the system weightier still, and both officials and general public suffer as a result. Moreover, it echoes pressure from the general public, and the two groups present a united front against any form of favoritism—so much so, finally, that the highest grades (and this is a curious paradox) are alone in their concern to humanize the machine.

Just as with the buffer-grade process, the process of rules and exceptions leads to noncommunication. Relations between petty officials and the general public are devoid of dependence, favoritism, or collusion, but this does not lead to rapid or more efficient arrangements. The system whereby the very dangerous power to make exceptions or "arrangements" is the exclusive preserve of the highest level paralyzes much of the administrative machine and, secondarily, overloads those at the top, with the result that senior officials are bogged down in routine detail.

Let us now move to a higher level and take a look at a very clearly marked opposition between the key national administrator—a director, or chief engineer, or prefect—who keeps all the local powers under his tutelage, and the local notable, particularly the mayor, who defends local liberties in the face of state encroachment.

The opposition between these two is in fact a purely rhetorical opposition. The actors, worlds apart socially, and officially opposed to each other in their public confrontations, are in fact highly considerate of each other's position and needs, since they depend heavily on one another for the successful fulfillment of their respective roles.

The mayor depends on the prefect, for example, because the prefect alone has the freedom to relax regulations that would otherwise paralyze him. He needs good access to his prefect because the prefect has the best information network in the *département*. Also, and above all, only the prefect can bestow upon him that official recognition which will make him a notable and which will consolidate his political position.

But the prefect in turn depends on the local powers, since he can achieve nothing alone. If he is to carry out the projects that will make his reputation as a man of action, it is essential that they allow him to manipulate them and that they agree not to disturb the general consensus. Both partners, finally, need to combine efforts in order to put pressure on the authorities in Paris.

Behind the apparent opposition, then, we find a deep complicity, resting on acceptance of the same values of order, stability, and harmony.* But this complicity creates a conservative blockage, since the dual manipulation in which the partners have to engage dilutes responsibility, brakes the decision-making process, and meanwhile makes it possible to evade all the difficult problems.

Another opposition, this time between the expert and the generalist, is more characteristic of the internal functioning of the government than it is of relations between the state and its citizens. The best example I have had the opportunity to analyze is that of relations between *polytechnicien* engineers and

* See Jean-Pierre Worms, "Le Préfet et ses notables," *Sociologie du travail*, March 1966.

the mechanical engineers employed in a state monopoly, a relationship I have described in *The Bureaucratic Phenomenon.*

The *polytechniciens* get the promotions, the official honors, and the theoretical power. The mechanical engineers, for their part, cannot move over to management and never receive anything more than seniority promotions within their categories. In all of the twenty or so factories I studied, the two groups were violently opposed, the *polytechniciens* accusing the mechanical engineers of being narrow-minded and arrogant, the engineers accusing their partners of being devoid of practical sense.

The origin of this conflict can be found at the conjunction between career situation and work situation. Frustrated in their careers, the engineers are advantageously placed where work is concerned, since they control the only source of uncertainty in an otherwise perfectly rationalized entity: maintenance and works. It is impossible to prevent them from using this power to block the *polytechniciens'* initiatives. Consequently, the latter, although they are the bosses, seem reasonably adjusted to their fate only when they resign themselves to impotence, while the engineers, constantly complaining that they are the ill-treated victims of the system, are highly satisfied. (The more satisfied, moreover, the more aggressive they are.)

This opposition has a deep effect on the decision-making machinery: the engineers, revolutionaries from a social standpoint, are extremely conservative in technical and organizational matters, since their power depends on the preservation of outdated practices; the *polytechniciens,* who are socially conservative, are, on the other hand, highly modernist in technical matters, since they see any form of reorganization as a means of regaining the upper hand over their opponents.

This results in total blockage. Each of the two groups possesses half of what is needed to transform an anachronistic situation. But they cannot cooperate. The superior, lacking relevant information, draws up plans that are too abstract. The subordinate, who is a master improviser, uses his gift to paralyze the superior, with whom he cannot otherwise compete. Members of both groups rarely escape from this determinism, where the impossibility of movement or any real exchange forces them to identify their personal interests with those of the group they belong to.

Of course, this is an exaggerated, though real enough example of an archetypal situation that can be found underlying all those caste conflicts which form the daily fabric of administrative life and which make any kind of evolution difficult.

Problems in the French Government Model

The French organizational system and bureaucratic style of action were valid responses to governmental problems in a society dominated by pre-industrial values. We may go even further and consider that the development of this system and style helped to perpetuate these values for longer than might otherwise have been the case. It is because they had this answer to their governmental problems that the French were able to cultivate that sense of the autonomy of the personality, that intellectual freedom, and that internal security which have for long characterized French civilization.

But if this is so, if French society and its administrative style really do live in profound symbiosis, the first conclusion that comes to mind is that, whatever its undesirable consequences, the system cannot be seriously disturbed, since it is the very expression of the society which it serves and of which it is at the same time the indirect reflection.

The argument would be irrefutable if the only purpose of a mode of action such as the French administrative style were to maintain the fundamental relations of the social system of which it was the expression. Of course this conservative function is essential, but it is not the only one. An organization and its style of action can only continue to exist if they also fulfill certain services and practical functions. We should look upon them as means and should assess them from an instrumental viewpoint, according to the results they give. Such an assessment is difficult to formulate for so vast an ensemble as an administrative agency, since its results are not really measurable, at least not directly. This is one of the reasons why, in all countries, public agencies have more marked national characteristics than other activities do. But the development of economics—and of rational calculation in general—has diminished this distinction. The shrinkage of the world, the interpenetration of societies, the opportunities for increased knowledge and comparisons make the practical consequences of any given method of action far clearer than in the past.

If, in this light, we look at the practical results of the French administrative system in terms of cost, we will quickly see that it is more and more obsolete. First, it fails to offer good possibilities of communication and participation and, consequently, cannot make effective use of its human and material resources; second, it adapts to change slowly and with great difficulty; lastly, it is a system tending to intellectual impoverishment and a loss of capacity for self-renewal and innovation.

The capacity to communicate is an essential condition for the good functioning of a modern organizational system. The system's efficiency depends more and more on its leaders' ability, on one hand, to ensure that they are informed of all the variables determining their decisions as quickly and precisely as possible, and, on the other hand, to inform their subordinates fully and rapidly of the objectives fixed by their decisions, the means to be employed, and the implied conditions of operation; in addition, they must be continually and precisely informed of the results of their decisions and of their subordinates' firsthand assessments. The spectacular improvement of communication techniques has greatly increased the possibilities here, but it would be a serious mistake to think that only technology is at issue. An organization can profit from the extraordinary potential of the new techniques only if it first eliminates the barriers that hamper frank communication among its various groups and hierarchical strata. The technological revolution merely serves to accentuate the distance between those organizations capable, for human reasons, of making effective use of its contributions and those whose internal social system makes them incapable of doing so.

French public agencies generally fall into the second category. When they do employ modern methods, these merely increase still further the volume of falsified communication; this naturally leads to paralysis. One cannot measure a system's capacity for communication on the basis of the volume of circulars, interdepartmental memoranda, or even processed statistical data. This sort of literature is little read because it has little relevance. It is used at all levels as a means of self-protection rather than as a means of information. And the agency involved generally finds itself in a vicious circle; the less it can get and circulate relevant information, the more it develops a process of misinformation, devaluing the notion of information and thus making it easier to turn one's back on real communication. The situation cannot improve so long as the human relations that determine the quality of communication remain unchanged and paralyzed—within the French administration, by traditional centralization and stratification. At a time when private business in all countries was dominated by a paternalism that was hardly propitious to communication, the French administrative style could pass for efficient; now, however, large corporations in most modern societies have discovered more liberal forms of government, as a result of which the inadequacies of the French style have begun to be apparent. And when technical progress seems to offer hitherto unsuspected opportunities for transformation, the French administration's inability to make up lost ground is going to be less and less tolerable.

The problem of the capacity for participation is of course closely related to that concerning the capacity for communication. This matter of participation is generally obscured because, as we have seen, it is generally discussed in moral terms. People want to get their subordinates to participate because that would mean introducing democracy into the company or agency, and because it is immoral to withhold from someone the right to concern himself in the affairs of the collectivity to which he belongs. But, as I have tried to show, the opportunities available for real participation appear that much better once one accepts that the right to participation, far from being a gift bestowed on inferiors for moral considerations, is a burden for them, one for which the leadership must be prepared to pay but which may eventually lead to the formation of something quite valuable. Every modern business relies increasingly on the good will of the people working for it, on their capacity for adaptation and innovation, and on their aptitude for mutual cooperation. The more complex the organization, the less it can function by simply applying the rules, the more it is forced to depend on the cooperation of its personnel, and the greater the efforts required from it to obtain the personnel's participation in the common enterprise.

However, the French administrative style does not favor this type of participation. Founded on rigid hierarchic principles, which in fact lead to a profound separation between "career"— a function of some mysterious essence distilled from the *grands concours**—and the accidental avatars of task and function, it neither encourages nor rewards participation. The distinction between those who think and those who execute remains fundamental. One can readily understand, then, why subordinates are reluctant to show enthusiasm, for this can only bring them trouble. The only kind of participation capable of growing within such a system is the one we have described as forced participation. The people concerned agree to take the initiative, but only on condition that they can then claim they were forced into it and that they are not responsible for it. This arrangement makes it possible to conceal many of the system's inadequacies, but it has some enormous disadvantages. First, it is a source of hidden privileges and advantages for subordinates, often more expensive for the administration than the rewarding of open participation. Second, it is effective only within rather narrow limits. And last but not least, it tends to block the system at a minimum level of participation, adequate for routine purposes

* See below, pp. 116–17.

but utterly inadequate when it comes to dealing with the continual transformations imposed by the modern environment.

Generally speaking, we may say that the French government administration mobilizes only a very small part of the human resources available to it. Here again, the acuteness of the problem is quite new, and we are a long way from seeing all its consequences. When industrial societies were still dominated by small organizations, and as long as nonparticipation of subordinates was the rule, the notion of the "glory and the servitude" of public service compensated for its stifling rules. But now that advanced countries are dominated by very large organizations, and now that these, despite their failings and shortcomings, have mobilized their members' capabilities by decentralizing operations and accepting limited but specific forms of dialogue and participation, the French administrative style will come to appear as archaic and oppressive as it already appears inefficient, unless it decides to reform itself.

Communication and participation would seem to be all the more necessary now that the problem of adjustment to change has become so urgent. Until now, the French bureaucratic system operated according to a mechanism of change through crisis. Incapable of self-correction after learning from its mistakes, it was forced to let problems accumulate to the point where a total transformation could permit resolution of its problems at one stroke—without endangering the fundamental equilibria between its groups and its members, which it is vital to preserve.

This kind of mechanism tends to turn reformers into authoritarian, charismatic personalities acting intuitively rather than rationally. Then, too, a crisis can hardly fail to arouse violent psychological reactions, subsequently leaving unpleasant memories. For all these reasons, this form of change undoubtedly helps to strengthen traditional resistance to change of any kind. Moreover, it is not very effective, since it usually acts blindly; the reformers are obliged to hide from all the interested parties so as to escape their various pressures; it is hard for them to check on their information or to experiment with new solutions.

Finally, and above all, while this mode of change may have been relatively well adapted to a slowly evolving society (like nineteenth-century bourgeois France), it is wholly inadequate to the accelerating pace of the world we now live in. After all, it was easy to accept a mechanism of change through crisis when one needed a crisis only every twenty years, or every generation. But this same mechanism becomes paralyzing when changes are necessary every five years. And it would be absurd to lay down absolute laws and settle everything at this speed forever.

So the French administrative model is becoming less and less rational. It is abstract, it stifles expression of the conflicts and needs of the society it serves, whose problems it understands less and less, and, despite its traditional emphasis on intellectual values, it is less and less capable of innovation and intellectual progress. It is a remarkable paradox: every effort is made to recruit France's most brilliant young men (for the system has the stiffest possible criteria for their selection); these people are then placed in privileged positions and protected from all forms of pressure, only to discover that they are prisoners of conservative modes of thought which, while allowing each man to shine, distract him from those innovative functions for which he was prepared.

In my opinion, this paradox may be explained by the degree to which the functions of the intellectual have been altered in the modern world. Nineteenth-century society tended radically to separate the world of ideas, in which thought could develop freely without bothering with practicalities it could not grasp, from the world of action, concerned with pragmatism or compromise and consequently held in lesser esteem. The transformation that has been taking place over the last twenty years, and whose first results are now becoming apparent, is tending to bridge this traditional gap. Society is becoming increasingly self-aware and conscious of its resources. We now refer less to principles that ought to determine our behavior, and are beginning rather to envisage ways in which the lessons of experience can help us to anticipate the future, instead of restricting action to what is dictated by the norms of the past.

This new awareness corresponds to the appearance of a new form of rationality. It can therefore be looked on as a kind of intellectual progress, and it is accompanied by new disciplines and new modes of thinking (operational research, games theory, econometrics, organization theory, cybernetics, systems analysis, et cetera). But it can develop fully only if it is accompanied by an equivalent transformation in the human relationships that surround intellectual research. The nineteenth-century intellectual was isolated and cut off from action, but the new-style intellectual must immerse himself in action (the results of which will provide him with vital matter for experiment); above all, he needs to work in an open milieu, one that permits confrontations across the frontiers of traditional disciplines and modes of thought. It is here that the compartmentalization of French society in general, and its administrative society in particular, is worst, and it is this that accounts for its backwardness, despite all the factors working in its favor.

The very unfortunate convergence that one finds in the French government, of education, membership in a particular corps, career prospects, and social position, makes for an almost insuperable conservative barrier. Modes of reasoning become corporative properties that cannot be questioned, since the careers of the members of the corps depend on them. The introduction of rational economic reasoning was delayed for fifteen years, despite a theoretical open-mindedness to it at the level of principles. It is not enough to transform, or even to revolutionize, administrative elites: the very system of human relations in which they are involved—in other words, the bureaucratic style—is at stake. So long as this style remains as it is, it will be impossible to make up for this intellectual backwardness. Moreover, the French administration is likely to find itself completely obsolete when accumulated experience (made possible by the development of new forms of action) enables us to move on to a further stage of intellectual reasoning. Progress does not stand still, and the French bureaucratic style, despite appearances, now prevents French society from keeping pace with it under satisfactory conditions.

The consequences of these shortcomings are likely to be even more serious in that the latent functions of the French administrative system and style—its psychological and social purposes—are losing their importance. It is not that people have less need of personal autonomy and intellectual freedom—quite the contrary—but these needs can now be met in other, less costly ways. Individuals will little resist utilitarian pressures in a society discontented with its present results, since they are more and more aware that alternative forms of organization can provide the protection they want.

The evolution of large modern organizations, indeed, does not seem to be tending toward the image of oppression and bureaucratization which is popularized in superficial analyses. Constant improvement in forecasting methods permits greater flexibility in the application of rules. Not as much conformity is needed in order to function. Advances in knowledge make it possible to relax the old constraints, since forecasts no longer need to rely on constraints to ensure their accuracy. At the same time, people are better trained than they were for work requiring cooperation. Personal autonomy and the guarantees the individual needed to protect himself from the risks of dependence are less important, since organizations can get the results they want without having to restrict individual liberty, and since people can cooperate effectively without the need for protection.

Of course, we are a long way from having thoroughly resolved this issue, but the bureaucratic model no longer appears quite so indispensable to the protection of the individual, and its ponderous rigidity seems to be that much more oppressive.

Similarities and Complementarities in French Society

There is no easy way out of the difficulties posed by the administrative model in its present impasse. We must take a further look at society as a whole, at its capacity for solving problems and for innovation.

I have said that a society can progress only so far as it is capable of inventing new styles of action that let it exploit the opportunities offered by general technological and economic developments. More concretely, its success depends upon its members' ability to cooperate effectively with a minimum of fuss; to create and preserve more complex organizations that will not be paralyzed by their own weight; and to make their society more open to innovation.

From this viewpoint, French society as a whole suffers from the same problems as its government bodies. The government's administrative style is no anomaly, and it lies at the heart of French collective life. For a long time now, the French have tried to downplay their problems by blaming everything on the government, and it all too easily becomes a scapegoat. Since the French are using a caricature of administrative reality when attacking it, realistic reforms become inconceivable, and indignation tends to become less effective as it becomes more violent. Indeed, we may perhaps say that the bureaucratic failings which the French so enjoy denouncing constitute that part of themselves which they are willing to criticize in order to defend their most ingrained habits more effectively against outside intrusion.

For it is true that the administrative style is central to all models of action and organization in French society. Although only a minority strictly adheres to it, analysis shows that even forms of behavior and practice farthest from it reveal underlying mechanisms similar, or at least complementary, to those of the state administration. This is to say that certain basic cultural traits manifest themselves throughout French life, and in the most varied situations. Two, especially, determine the style of action adopted: one, a fear of face-to-face relations that may lead to conflict or situations of dependence and that threaten the individual's autonomy; the other, an absolutist conception of authority without which it is impossible for a Frenchman to imagine the successful undertaking of even the most trivial collective action.

There is an obvious contradiction between the two tendencies. The French are terrified of situations where they are likely to be dependent, but at the same time they are incapable of conceiving of a collectivity that has no strong authority. As a result, they cannot support the very authority they consider to be indispensable.

Of course, contradictions in human relationships do not have to be resolved, nor are they necessarily a cause of failure. In fact, a society's characteristic style of action or mode of government develops around them. The survival of a bureaucratic style is associated in France with the permanence of these contradictory tendencies. Absolute and arbitrary authority is preserved in principle and as a final, reassuring resort; centralization, which keeps this authority at a safe distance, and stratification, which protects the individual from it, help to render it harmless. This obviates face-to-face relations and the risks of dependence and conflict, while individual autonomy is safeguarded without giving free reign to disorder or anarchy.

The bureaucratic organizational mode and style of action account for only part of reality, however. Despite constant improvements being made in the system, it cannot eliminate arbitrariness. Parallel powers grow up alongside it; privileges are constantly getting established in the interstices of the official construct.

As against the formal bureaucratic law, "system D" * permits all needed adjustments to be made. It is the law's living, constant, and indispensable antithesis—indeed, one wonders sometimes whether this seamy side is not perhaps the more closely woven texture. In any case, it is this opposition which one finds in the model of evolution followed by French society, whose main characteristic is the primacy of the crisis mechanism.

Crisis, as a privileged means of bringing about change, may indeed be considered as the basic cultural trait conditioning the

---

* An expression dating from World War I: *Le Français est débrouillard*, or, "The French are good improvisers."

Frenchman's favorite style of collective action. In the strategy of human relations to which the French are accustomed, this style is characterized by a deep and constant opposition between the individual and the group: the group is perceived and experienced as an organ for defense and protection whose activities can only be negative, while it is for the individual himself to find new means of self-assertion.

Creative individual assertion is made easier by the group's protection, which ensures complete independence and psychological freedom for the individual; but such individual assertion is opposed by the group insofar as it might lead to constructive action, thus threatening the status quo. On the other hand, the individual, who observes continually the undesirable effects of the over-rigid system imposed by various group pressures, is completely free to criticize an organization whose shortcomings are obvious where he is concerned. The system, for its part, can withstand a good deal of criticism of this sort over a long period, since the same individual, an ardent innovator when speaking in the abstract and as an individual (as an intellectual), reverts to conservatism when he comes to act as member of a group. The alternation of long periods of routine with short bursts of crisis, which can be observed in the history of both public and private institutions and organizations, is the natural consequence of this mechanism. And another consequence is the radical totalitarian character of whatever demands for change do occur, as well as the permanence of a revolutionary tradition that makes any kind of experimentation impossible and that makes recourse to (or creation of) a higher authority necessary, especially in times of crisis.

I need hardly emphasize that this condensed analytic scheme should be considered as nothing more than a rough sketch highlighting, by its very exaggerations, certain deepseated characteristics we could not otherwise perceive. Obviously, it explains only certain latent tendencies in French society and certain specific blockage mechanisms. But these mechanisms are very real, and we must not underestimate their consequences. Many of the problems paralyzing French collective life are related to them. For example:

1. The very great difficulties, which Tocqueville had already noted more than a century and a half ago, in launching any kind of cooperative activity or any living and constructive group or association (collective gatherings are rarely more than defense organs).

2. The inability of most groups or institutions to manage conflicts in an evolutionary and dynamic manner. They either stifle the conflicts or allow them to reach the point of explosion.

3. The general reluctance, both in business and in public administration, to accept the reality of human relationships. While no society can tolerate total clarity in this area, the confusion so skillfully maintained over the issue of responsibility is nevertheless characteristic of modern French society.

4. The great difficulty encountered in all domains when attempting to develop flexible organizations capable of rapid adjustment and innovation. Whatever the intentions, once the first enthusiasm has worn off, it is hard to avoid relapsing into the complementary rigidities of the bureaucratic or paternalistic models.

5. The preservation and development of a sterile and in some ways artificial conflict between the public and private domains. The public authorities, which are suspicious of private activities *a priori*, assume the right to orient them; those in charge of private activities protest against state control but never hesitate to profit from a monopolistic situation or the restriction of competition which the state creates; they extract a heavy price from the collectivity for the privileges which the state is forced to accord them. In sum, the artificial conflict between blind *dirigisme* and a not very enterprising free enterprise serves primarily to maintain the status quo.

6. The isolation of sectors of activity, functions, castes, milieus, and various ideological families in so many closed corporations, making these human groupings rigid, frail, and inefficient. Since negotiations and exchanges are practicable

only at the highest level, mistrust paralyzes all forms of innovative action; this institutional paralysis blocks evolution in the workers', peasants', and small shopkeepers' worlds. Leaders are unable to compromise, since they are closely watched by their militant supporters, who set themselves up as watchdogs of the ideology which is created in these isolated worlds and which is used to justify them. Collective action is bogged down in the quicksands of state centralization, and the crippling inability of society as a whole to make integrative comparisons, except at the highest level and in the most formal way, makes public life congested at the top and bloodless at the base.

Of course, all societies have their vicious circles and their rigidities. The recurring behavioral traits encountered in French society, some of them since before the Revolution, have counterparts in all European societies. Even American society, while more flexible, more open to communication, more apt for development, is not exempt. All the same, we can reasonably assert that the problems are far more acute, and consequently emerge more clearly, in contemporary French society, since it has suffered longer from stagnation—perhaps because of the relative perfection of the model of civilization it had succeeded in creating in the past.

At all events, the French model of bureaucratic protection and change-through-crisis is now seen to be increasingly costly and inefficient.

In the economic sphere, it makes it difficult to concentrate production units (except in sectors where standardization is easily achieved), it hampers business adaptability, and it favors well-established activities and fortunes at the expense of new men and innovators. Of course, France has managed to preserve its living standards at a high level equal to that of its major European rivals without any decisive changes in its organizational system or style of action, by pushing administrative centralization and social and economic protectionism to extreme lengths. But it paid dearly for this, in the nineteenth and early twentieth centuries, by a loss of national substance, which fell to half that of England or Germany,* and by a lag in "organizational" capacity that is harder and harder to make up.

In the social sphere, it favors conservative activities while harshly penalizing any attempts at innovation or assumption of responsibility.

In the intellectual sphere, while it protects creative intellectual ferment, it does so at the expense of experimentation, which for a long time now has been the predominant form of scientific development.†

And in the political sphere, it tends to stifle the real conflicts, so that the political process is bogged down in artificial conflicts through which no innovation nor institutional progress can be achieved.

The Lessons of the Recent Past

If, as I have tried to show, French society really is blocked, is it possible for it to change, and how could it change?

Change is not, in fact, ineluctable. There is no automatic response to technological evolution. New conditions do not necessarily lead to better-adapted forms of organization. History is full of examples of groups and societies stagnating for long periods with inefficient models that nonetheless let them preserve their traditions and identity.

Even if, in the case of French society, we were to set aside the hypothesis of the autarchy of structures and behavioral models, and of the decline that could not fail to accompany it, we can conceive of two types of change: the passive adoption of elements from foreign, especially American, models; and the

* While the Frenchman's standard of living was growing as fast as that of his English or German neighbors in the last hundred years, this performance was achieved with a stagnant population, while neighboring countries doubled their populations. This tendency has been reversed in the past twenty-five years.

† The relative backwardness of French science is due not to intellectual inferiority but to the French scientific community's narrowness, and to its bureaucratic and corporate structures.

active development of a new model based on the experience of both successes and mistakes. To understand the real possibilities available here, we must first understand the changes that have occurred in the last twenty-five years, many of which would have seemed improbable before World War II. France has moved from a stagnant economy to a growth economy; behavior in both business and government has altered; economics have taken precedence over politics; preoccupation with ideology has lessened; traditional chauvinism and nationalism are gradually fading away; and such deeply ingrained patterns as demographic Malthusianism seem to have been reversed.

The crisis of May 1968 demonstrated that these new phenomena had their limits, however. Economic development suddenly appeared vulnerable; the demonstrators' violent return to ideological passion reversed the trend to reformism and "economism," and the new fashion among the young looked as if it would drag them, and the rest of us, back to the religious debates of the pre-industrial era. Yet the May explosion was, ambiguously but profoundly, also the true revolt against France's bureaucratic mode of organization and against the authoritarian aspects of the French style.

A more intensive analysis of the processes of change already under way is thus indispensable if we want to obtain a true empirical picture of what is going on, rather than resting content with theatrical declarations and statistical figures. This analysis does not yet exist, for French society's self-awareness is still very limited. But we can at least discuss some of the signs of change that have appeared in the areas of communication, leadership, forms of action, and forms of organization. What is striking is that more constructive forms of collective action *have* appeared in these areas, many of whose manifestations were completely unexpected.

Let us consider the example offered by rural France. At the time of the Liberation, in 1944, it was possible to foresee that the exodus from France's rural villages would accelerate, but no one dreamed of suggesting that the French peasant would respond to this natural pressure other than by passive resistance and sporadic agitation. And indeed we are mainly made aware of apparently irresponsible attitudes and behavior—the agricultural lobbies' demagogy, echoes of *jacqueries* of the past in road barricades and assaults on local government officials. But a careful, objective look at the situation, and a serious comparison between present forms of collective action and those which prevailed before the war, will show that rural France has undergone a considerable mutation. The overall response of the rural milieu has been marked by longer-term collective campaigns—which suggests that responsible leaders and activists have appeared who are establishing constructive goals: technical and economic training, technical and commercial research and experiment, discussion of the structure of the milieu. These activities could develop only as a result of considerable collective action, mobilizing thousands of people and directly or indirectly affecting hundreds of thousands more.

It was hard to foresee such an awakening of the peasant masses, and in fact no one did foresee it. Social groups that had felt and perceived themselves only passively, or at least defensively, suddenly sought to take their fate into their own hands. This effort was not free of a heavy dose of romanticism and illusion, but at the grass roots, at the countless meetings where young farmers tried to understand and master their environment, a new style of action had appeared. Behind these attempts at self-education lay a whole process of coming to terms with others, of initiation into activities aimed at collective advancement.

Of course, this style of action cannot resolve technical and economic problems; the enthusiasm for group agriculture is merely the froth on a wave whose economic and political effect may be somewhat dubious, at least to begin with. But nonetheless the great rural exodus, which destroyed the equilibrium of French society and will continue to disturb it until the traditional peasantry has completely disappeared, is not going to occur in the disintegrative climate one might have feared—at least not in many regions. Meanwhile, the appearance of new collective resources within the most conservative sector of

French society offers the entire country an opportunity for considerable development.

We can analyze similar transformations in the Catholic world in the same light. (It has not been the marginal or peripheral sectors of French society that have changed over the past twenty years as was the case in preceding decades, but the most traditional milieus, the cornerstones of the social order.) Despite political resistance and social disturbance, the Church's base has shifted, principally because of a new style of action involving altered modes of participation and leadership. This transformation has been going on longer and more gradually than the peasant awakening (of which it was partly the source), but it is moving in the same direction. The paternalism of the past has not wholly disappeared, but the capacity for initiative and commitment, for open-mindedness and militant action, has changed completely.

This change in the style of human relations, which can be seen in many other fields as well, has been accompanied by a far greater openness to contacts and exchanges between groups. The old partitioning of professions, parties, and ideological orientations* seems to be declining. We may make fun of the sudden fad for "dialogue" and "communication"; professions of faith are all too often restricted to words alone, and we lack the means to measure the progress actually accomplished; all we can do is to take note of the failures, such as failed attempts at political reform. But progress has certainly been made, in that religious affiliation is no longer a pertinent barrier, political allegiances no longer provoke visceral hatreds, and the hostility between the public and private sectors has greatly diminished. Slowly French society is abandoning the religious wars that formed one of the foundations of its system of government and one of the justifications of its bureaucratic order.

The success enjoyed by new modes of organization naturally seems to be much less broad. This touches a more complex level of change, one that implies the restructuring of the entire range

* The usual phrase in the 1940s and 1950s was *familles spirituelles.*

of human relations in organizations. Those who take a strict functionalist line on social phenomena see changes in organizational modes as the consequences of something, not as a motive force in themselves, and they argue that new organizational modes can emerge only when society's values change. This is not my view. I think, on the contrary, that change cannot occur on the level of values alone but only if inventions and innovations are made at the level of praxis, for the purpose of dealing with a critical situation. Of course inventions and innovations are shaped by limits created by the present system of values. But the system of values may be modified, in turn, by transformed organizational modes and styles of action. The practical success of new modes of organization may therefore have consequences of a general order. Human groups can learn from action—a sort of natural form of experimentation for them. The rigidity of the social system has yet to adjust to this.

It may be true that most employees in the private sector continue to be dominated by traditional paternalist or bureaucratic modes, but the private sector nonetheless seems to be open to experiment and capable of assimilating examples of experimental success. The spread of American ideas about organization is certainly messy, and borrowings from the model are often incoherent. But a new attitude, open to organizational innovation, is clearly emerging. Management consultants are gradually abandoning the Taylorian model of which French engineers such as Fayol and Bedeaux had been important exponents. Practitioners are far ahead of the traditional French teachers of this subject: the Harvard Business School is beginning to enjoy greater prestige than the Ecole Polytechnique. Even if the overliteral and badly understood borrowings occur more often than does an active, empirical elaboration of organizational modes genuinely corresponding to true needs, a real movement is now under way whose leaders are actually capable of learning from experience.

Institutional Learning Processes

To the description of each of these developments one can counter pessimistic remarks about the resistance of the milieu and the limited range of real successes. French businesses, from the point of view of international competition, may appear badly handicapped by obsolescence, the organizational causes of which are rarely understood. But the same developments seem rather promising if we look at them as early stages of a learning process leading to new forms of organization.

Change itself—at least such change as we are able to observe—generally seems ambivalent, for it often uses traditional mechanisms, and it is hard to decide whether the change strengthens or transcends them. For example, it is at the very moment when farmers at last become active and commit themselves to constructive action that barricades spring up across the roads and the traditional defense of rural interests becomes most demagogic. Or again, planning—which served as an instrument for progress in the management world, forcing employers to face up to their collective responsibilities and accustoming them to adapt to new rationalities—was done using all the old channels of collusive interests, bolstering the old *dirigiste* dreams and prolonging their influence.

Let us tackle the problem the other way around. Instead of trying to work out which direction evolution is taking, and weighing each new development in terms of the trend we consider most "progressive," we should ask what issues face French society as a result of the development of a more efficient style of action and mode of organization.

This issue is one of learning processes, in the sense psychologists now give to this term in experimental usage: how can a new form of behavior, one that provides a satisfactory answer to the problem the subject has to deal with, be really adopted by him? The learning process thus conceived is not a passive molding process, such as is used when one sets out to "teach" something to someone in the traditional educational system; it is an intensive, innovating process. Obviously, neither a group nor an organization can learn in the same way a person does. But if psychology began to make great advances the moment it started to reason in terms of learning processes, then sociology too can gain by studying the process of change from a similar angle—that is, emphasizing not so much the end results or the motivations of change, but rather the conditions for restructuring a complex system as a function of both the survival problems the system will have to face and the desirable or undesirable sanctions that the environment will mete out.

From this point of view we are justified in saying that French society's capacity for integration is too weak, and the possibilities of measuring results and perceiving environmental reactions are far too confused, for even the most undifferentiated learning process to develop. A society so complex can only really learn at the level of its intermediate structures. But here French society's capacity for learning is limited by the relative lack of autonomy not only of political and territorial units, but also of many economic units.

Indeed, all sorts of pressures are at work in French society to restrict opportunities for real experiment in the basic groups and organizations. In the administrative and educational sectors these amount to virtual prohibitions. In the political sphere, openings are so limited that risk-taking is unthinkable. It is much easier to experiment in the business world, but so many factors have to be regarded as constraints—restrictive bank credit, protected markets, a rigid employment situation, the absence of a market for senior executives—that innovation is frequently looked on as a dangerous risk.

Speaking very generally, the French social system is still stratified, hierarchized, and compartmentalized, while its workings are still controlled enough for it to be possible to penalize innovations that might upset society's order and stability.

France's very poor learning capacity stems from the defensive, cautious strategy imposed on most of its operational units—which alone are capable of coming up with innovations.

If we try to understand how these constraints develop, we find three main systems of control:

1. The administrative system, closely controlling all public collective activities, which is increasingly important in the development process and which influences, directly or indirectly, the greater part of the private sector of the economy.

2. The educational system, which largely controls all the selection mechanisms upon which promotion and career success are based, and which therefore is an integral part of the system of stratification, hierarchy, and compartmentalization.

3. The political system, which holds the monopoly on the integration of collective activities right at the very top of the system, and therefore (hand in glove with the administrative system) forbids all integrative activity at intermediate levels— thus robbing vitality from units otherwise capable of innovation.

Of course French society is continually experimenting. But each party jealously guards the secrets of its experiments, since the governing strategy requires secrecy and self-defense. Certain circumstances and certain irresistible movements favor cooperative learning processes, and then the rapidity with which they catch on becomes a matter for astonishment; but these tend to come too little and too late to solve the kinds of problem whose dimensions and urgency gave rise to the movements in the first place. It is very rarely possible, in sectors as important as those which are now blocked and in trouble, to build up enough critical mass to tip the balance.

Not surprisingly, in these circumstances the people involved are rapidly discouraged. Everyone tries to utilize within his own system whatever he has managed to achieve. Young Turks become local bigwigs, and reforming leaders become corporatists. When breakdown finally occurs, it creates disarray rather than change. Each man shuts himself up in his own ideal of workers' control (*autogestion*), preferring to resolve all problems in the absolute world of daydreams to transforming the real conditions of the process.

Worse still, this is likely to lead to regression, since this disintegration undermines the slow and difficult progress made in the learning process, slowing down the forces working for change by closing them in the vicious circle of protest.

Does this mean that we are condemned forever to lose the fruits of such progress as we do achieve? Things are not so simple. Should we then conclude that the crisis of breakdown, like all learning processes and like all processes of change, is ambivalent? To give a slightly better answer to this question, first we must take a more serious look at the French model of ferment and protest, of which the crisis of May 1968 provided such a good example.

CHAPTER SIX

The Collapse of the University

The French university offers an excellent example of the themes we have discussed in French society. The collapse of the university, a typically bureaucratic community, expressed the profound uneasiness of the entire French system, while at the same time the crisis it underwent reinforced its own basic characteristics.

Nowhere were the retrogressive aspects of the revolutionary movement of 1968 more evident. This is because the university's "suffocating Napoleonic centralization" is a characteristic not simply grafted onto an otherwise healthy body—whether on purpose or just unluckily—but integral to the university, expressing its philosophy and mode of being. To eliminate it root and branch, or even simply to create the conditions for lessening it, would require a fundamental alteration of the entire university.

The essential characteristic of the French university system—and the reason for its solidarity—is that around its institutional skeleton it has developed an intellectual style or, if one prefers, mode of reasoning, a type of teaching (or of human relations), and a relationship with the rest of society that reinforce and sustain it. Each of these elements has an underlying logic, which makes it highly resistant in its own right, but they are also interdependent, and together they make the university structure apparently unshakable.

Monopoly is the basic thing: the system does not tolerate any competition. There can only be one university, one faculty, one school per geographical area; one could easily imagine that there should never be more than one teacher per discipline or subdiscipline in any one place. Monopoly means compulsory curricula, captive audiences, and the rejection of any outside interference or influence in the running of the university.

Centralization is the natural and virtually inevitable counterpart of monopoly. Setting up this immense army so that all its units are equal and all are equally dependent on the summit seems utterly absurd, of course. But it is the least bad way of maintaining a minimum of efficiency and cohesion, in an agency which isolation from the external world and lack of internal competition have made so conservative. In fact, innovators tend to gather at the top, and their activities generally lead to further excessive centralization.

The university's intellectual style, closely related to this organizational model, plays a considerable part in shoring it up. Clarity, stability, formal rigor, abstract and deductive modes of reasoning—all these typically French qualities express the university's organizational mode and are the conditions of its survival. Centralization requires a uniform and standardized universe, formalism is essential to bureaucratic order, while abstract and deductive reasoning ensures its protection against the outside world.

The French university teaching style is based on a certain distance maintained between master and pupil, and on the assumption of superior intellectual power on the teacher's part—he possesses the truth (the consequences and condition of the deductive mode of reasoning). The negative response which this elicits (protest and rowdyism) makes it all the more necessary to keep a certain distance and protection between teachers and pupils. The lecture course (*cours magistral*) symbolizes this relationship and at the same time expresses the prevailing intellectual style; it is an essential part of the prevailing organizational mode. Among the students, it makes for a vicious circle of passivity and protest.

The university's relation to the rest of society is founded upon the absolute primacy of selection, which is seen as the primary function of education. French society is an ascriptive society,* where examinations and competitions take the place of birthright. Its social mission is to accomplish the feat of preserving the traditional social hierarchy while ensuring equal opportunity for all in the educational sphere, and to provide the necessary training for those who enter the socially most prestigious professions.

The primacy of the selection function ensures the educational system's power, as well as that of its members, and it is around this function that the power mechanisms making up its regulatory apparatus have developed. Consequently, the processes of experimental learning are devalued, and the effort to make contact with the outside world is proscribed, while abstract programs and deductive methods are justified. University and society always live symbiotically, but they can do so either in an atmosphere of continual and fertile exchange or in relative and sterile isolation. The mechanism of French-style symbiosis allows the university community to isolate itself from society and at the same time to impose some of its norms on society.

As a result, the university is impervious to change. It is blind to the outside world. It can neither adapt to the changing environment nor even perceive it. To modify the curriculum is to jeopardize the career prospects and the power of the teachers. To change teaching methods and human relations is to upset the organization, and, in any case, organizational change is blocked by the teachers and the conflict between different bodies sharing power within the university.

---

* That is, a society in which each person is assigned a place and function, not according to what he has achieved or seems capable of achieving but in terms of his status and rank of origin.

The Mechanisms of Crisis

For France's university system, the crisis of May 1968 was total, questioning everything at once with a brutality as sudden as it was unexpected—the lecture-course system, human relations in the schools, the content of the cultural message imparted, the organizational system, and the way students are selected—because nothing could really change in a system whose elements were so closely interdependent unless everything changed at the same time. The totally integrated system provoked total contestation. Resurgence of a chiliastic and totalitarian ideology was a natural consequence of the crisis rather than its cause—even if, at another level, this ideology was a motive force in the "revolution."

At the same time, the totality of the challenge and the extremes to which it led tended to paralyze the movement of revolt, binding it to the system so that it became a kind of reverse caricature of it. As if demonstrated in a laboratory experiment, the crisis thus revealed one of the paradoxes of the bureaucratic system which I believed I had observed in my previous studies of French administrative agencies.

As with any bureaucratic system, the university can change only through crisis. Crisis is a temporary breakdown of the bureaucratic order, but it does not entail its destruction. It is simply an interlude of mobile warfare between very long periods of trench warfare, an interlude in the course of which individuals can give free rein to creative and irresponsible impulses, while the negative and conservative behavior of institutionalized hierarchic groups and categories temporarily disappears. But once the period of structural fusion is over, the need and the general love of ordered, planned, and regularized situations quickly calls a new bureaucratic order into being, which is nothing more than the old order better adjusted to the demands of the environment.*

* See Crozier, *The Bureaucratic Phenomenon*, pp. 286–93.

Four years after the events, we can say that the mechanisms of the May 1968 crisis have so far corresponded perfectly to this theoretical pattern. Will the final outcome give the French a system differing from the old one only in that it is better adapted to new material needs? This would be the natural law of the bureaucratic universe, and no reformer, whether cabinet minister or student, can afford to underestimate its power. Yet even if this logic seems confirmed, it is still worth pondering whether a deeper and more basic transformation of the French university system did not begin during those painful experiences. Such a transformation would seem inevitable, given the now open divorce between the university world and society at large, and the difficulty in finding a lasting solution that is not prejudicial to the French university style of action and mode of government.

From this point of view, four issues, which correspond to the elements of the system I have briefly summarized, seem to be particularly important: the problem of the university's style of human relations; the problem of general culture; the problem of the place of the new petit-bourgeois strata in society; the problem of selection of elites and preservation of higher castes.

Human Relations

The student revolt of 1968 was directed with the greatest violence against the traditional university's style of human relations. The collective hysteria that was essential to the launching of the revolutionary movement developed through a series of experiments in human relations that were radically new—at least for the participants.

The *enragés* on the Nanterre campus of the university of Paris who suddenly emerged around the figure of Daniel Cohn-Bendit effectively managed, for at least a moment in the paroxysm of their revolt, to square the circle of direct democracy: they created a crowd in which individuals could express themselves, an action without organization, permanent spontaneity, all of it open and good-natured.

This was possible, of course, only in a kind of delirium, like that of the patient who resolves his contradictions in sleepwalking. It was dangerous, moreover, since this wave of tolerance, aimed at full expression and liberation of instinct, could be maintained only in the context of absolutist rigor, imposing real psychological terror on everyone. And in this extreme movement, this anti-discourse, we can see the same desperate passion for total, contradiction-free speech that animates the charismatic passion of the *discours magistral.*

Was there any genuine innovation in these experiments? Did the encounters and conversions illuminating those spectacular *prises de paroles* have any concrete consequences? We should be careful about this. It was not the first time that revolutionaries have acted out the most spontaneous informality before establishing a Caesarean formalism.

Still, I am inclined to think that the extraordinary psychodrama did in fact help people move away, at the immediately reflexive human level at least, from a formalism that no longer fitted with the spirit of the times. I also believe that, after this shock, people became less satisfied with the background purring of the *cours magistral* and responded to it less passively. But in a situation like this, accommodations to tradition are all too likely—since what is being sought is the ecstasy of communion, the harmony of integration, not the capacity to tolerate conflicts and confront truth head-on. Sociologists who have analyzed techniques of human relations are well aware that this is an area that is prone to manipulation, and one does not need the evil intrusion of monopoly capitalism to get caught up in it. The changes that actually did occur or that can be expected are not necessarily incompatible with the bureaucratic order, then; they may even furnish it with a new basis.

One may ask, though, whether a less spectacular but more decisive long-term process may not have been set in motion, going beyond the confines of the university and involving that part of the intellectual world which is concerned with science and action.

The traditional relations of French society have especially hampered original research and intellectual activities, because, as I have said, an essential condition for innovation is not only individual creativity but a cooperative supporting environment, which alone makes it possible to try out new ideas immediately and experiment with the solutions they offer. The violence of the chain reactions set off by the student revolt of 1968 led to the disintegration of at least some of the old constraining structures. In some ways the situation still looks depressing, but perhaps it now offers an opportunity for a much-needed clean sweep.

General Culture

Culture is no longer a useless luxury reserved for a privileged minority of aristocrats and marginal creators. It has come to be an essential tool of action in a rationalized world that can be mastered only by using modes of reasoning that require a certain cultural apprenticeship.

But different forms of culture do not have equal educational value. The French university preserved a classical, rationalist, and humanist cultural tradition which, despite its continuing prestige, became wholly inadequate to the contemporary world. I am speaking not only of the cult of the classical humanities, but far more generally of the modes of reasoning inculcated in legal studies, physics and mathematics, and history. The narrowest kind of rationalism still dominates all these fields, and the only things that have been offered in place of it are anticipatory dreams so ambitious that they are accepted as religions rather than used as tools for learning.

Modernist reformers, usually concerned with immediate needs, attack classical culture while failing to put anything in its place. They have yet to discover that the demand for general culture is stronger today than ever before, and that precisely because of this demand our classical culture *must* be transformed. Modern man is in far greater need than his predecessors were of the intellectual tool, which remains when all else has been forgotten, for it provides its possessor with a grip on the world and enables him to make active and experimental use of all the knowledge he may subsequently acquire.

Paradoxically, American universities today offer a better general cultural training than does that temple of classicism, the Sorbonne. The last French attempt at modernization before 1968, the Fouchet reform, pushed narrow specialization to extreme limits. How could this regressive approach have been thought acceptable? Essentially because it permitted an acceleration in the vital technical updating of the subjects being taught. Scientific progress had deeply affected certain subjects without touching the traditional *lycée* complex—literature-mathematics-philosophy—which formed the university's classical base and around which its principal vested interests had entrenched themselves.*

The revolt of May 1968 was also an expression of rebellion among students caught in this dilemma: formalist classical culture or narrow specialization? This accounts for the incoherence of their demands—some calling for a more concrete, professionally oriented education, others asking that they be given theoretical training worthy of their intellectual powers. The romantic will to total knowledge and to total revolution that frequently emerged during 1968 was a natural and perfectly understandable escapism in the face of this contradiction. But at the same time it made truly realistic understanding impossible.

The Petite Bourgeoisie and the Elites

The greatest difficulty in resolving these contradictions, however, stems from another dimension of the problem—its social and power dimension.

---

* So long as university power is centered on the traditional competitive exams, called *agrégations*, which give entry to the best university careers, there is no chance of a renewal of classical culture.

If new forms of human relations are to be explored and amplified, if the many germs of the new general culture are to take root in favorable soil, then teachers and students and society's innovative elites must find a common ground—which is not easy, since the system has radically separated the various groups that should collaborate.

The student revolt was not, in fact, a revolution of the culturally most advanced parts of the student world. To a large extent it was a petit-bourgeois revolt, a revolt of the new social strata for whom the affluent society gave access to university culture.

In France the university system and the technocratic elite had completely ignored the influx of this enormous new mass of people, because the only areas that really mattered to them—the *grandes écoles*, selection through the *grands concours*, and the preservation of the accompanying privileges—were left untouched by them.* At heart the French establishment was uninterested in the university faculties; it has its own separate recruitment and educational system. On top of this, most serious research was done outside the university, and the latter

---

* In terms of prestige the *grandes écoles* dominate the French educational system. These include the *Ecole Polytechnique* (the alumni are called *polytechniciens*), where the training is oriented to engineering; the *Ecole Nationale d'Administration* (E.N.A.; its alumni are called *énarques*), responsible for training civil servants; the *Ecole Normale Supérieure*, which prepares students for the *agrégation*, the highest and most prestigious qualification in the teaching profession; the *Ecole Centrale*; the *Ecole des Mines*, which trains engineers for the principal technical posts. These *écoles* are run by the ministries responsible for the respective careers to which they lead; thus the *Polytechnique* is administered by the Ministry of Defense and is run as a military establishment (though few students actually take up careers in the Army), while the *Ecole Nationale d'Administration* is administered by the Prime Minister's office.

The *grandes écoles* lead to careers in the *grands corps*: the *Conseil d'Etat*, the *Inspectorat des Finances*, diplomacy, prefectorial administration, mining corps, roads and bridges corps, et cetera. Many members of the *grands corps* subsequently get jobs in the private sector of industry (known as *pantouflage*) or in politics.

Entrance to the *grandes écoles* is by competition (the *grands concours*). Despite this seeming meritocracy, the competitions tend to select candidates from a fairly narrow range of social classes.

played little or no scientific role other than through the activities of teachers who worked in outside institutes as well. It is easy to see why the climate of the university and the quality of its teaching continued to deteriorate for so long. Protests naturally arose among the people who discovered, painfully, that they had been made fools of, and that the higher education which was supposed to enable them to move up the social ladder* was little more than a period spent in a cultural factory where they were fed nothing but piecemeal knowledge, with mediocre career prospects at the end.

These problems are common to all Western countries, but no other country has organized social selection through the educational process so severely and so humiliatingly as France. No other society has squandered so much human potential so indifferently, nor sought to hide its conservatism behind such demagogic egalitarianism. This situation is what gave the French student revolt its large social dimension and led to its making such a striking impact upon the conscience of France. But the special combination of a thirst for novelty and change and an expression of sectional interests on the part of the petite bourgeoisie that occurred there is more likely to lead us back to the bureaucratic quagmire than toward renewal of any kind.

The line of least resistance would be to satisfy the petit-bourgeois demands by allowing them easier access to the bureaucratic order, without at the same time touching the pillars of the social order: the *grandes écoles* and the *grands concours*. Since no selection system can be introduced in the universities, and since there is no chance of relaxation in the ferocious selection system of the *grands concours*† (now more or less unique in the world), the chasm can only widen between the two natural

---

* The university faculties recruit members of the establishment who have fallen by the wayside; their frustration at having lost their chance in the great meritocratic process of the *grandes écoles* is all the more violent for knowing exactly the significance of their failure.

† The French do not seem bothered by this paradoxical coexistence of the most elitist system alongside the most egalitarian one.

elements of the French system—on one hand, management, shaped by the tough apprenticeship of the career system, and on the other, the ordinary mass of white-collar workers, left to *laissez faire* and to their own devices. The *grandes écoles,* despite their obsolescence, will thus continue to be considered indispensable to maintain that minimum of competence without which no one could carry out a prestigious function efficiently.

Even if it were decided to organize the career prospects of the university's petit bourgeois, it would be only to put them in their place—that is, at a much lower level, where there would be no chance of their competing with, or threatening, the monopolies of the traditional castes. This approach, which was implicit in the post-1968 reform, is very likely to be dangerous both for the university and for society. The gulf separating an extremely restricted elite from the middle classes (without whom the elite cannot function) will widen at the very time when a broadening of the governing strata and the liberalization of the social process would seem to be essential for developing society's creativity. Meanwhile, middle-level executives and technicians, now a very crucial group, will become more and more frustrated at finding themselves left outside the main career system, and will seek consolation in bureaucratic resistance and recrimination, still further crippling an already half-paralyzed society. And, finally, the university community will be unable to change and reform if it can provide neither the pressure of competition (which one does not find in the hierarchized *grandes écoles,* the universities, or teaching and research units) nor the yeast of research, nor the attractions of success, nor those contacts with the outside world that come from adjusting curricula to actual needs and caring for the students' job market.

The core problem of the university's renewal thus seems to be the selection of elites, the preservation of the mandarin classes and the traditional governing circles, based on and reinforced by the *grandes écoles.*

The great importance of the *grandes écoles* in French society is not merely that they train future members of the elite, but that they give rise to the elitist phenomenon itself, endowing it with its basic characteristics in personnel, degree of openness, and relations with other rival or "subordinate" groups.

When students at the *Ecole Nationale d'Administration* say they are interested in power, they are telling the television interviewer what he expects to hear, since he has managed to make incarnate in them a myth (of which they are as much the prisoners as beneficiaries), but at the same time they are expressing a decisively important reality. This reality requires dispassionate analysis. Elites emerge in all societies—that is, we see in all societies the development of managerial circles linked by a network of cooperative and rival relations based on complicity and protection. No system is good in itself, but a society's capacity for development and innovation is heavily influenced by the procedures whereby it selects elites.

The French system of selection—an extremely severe, impersonal, precocious one based on a strict assessment of intellectual qualities developed in intensive training—offers, along with certain advantages that were once important in the past, a number of disadvantages that are increasingly making themselves felt. The advantages are that it permits younger men to rise rapidly to the top and facilitates communication among people with responsibilities in a wide range of institutions, sectors, and professions. But there are disadvantages. The opportunities for power presented to the privileged group constitute, if not a monopoly, at least a form of rent which its possessors consider they are duty-bound to preserve and hand on to new members. The homogeneity of the selection and training process leads to mutual confidence and to the development of a common language—both very useful for speeding up business, but also accentuating the elite's deep mistrust of outsiders and creating barriers that protect the group but reduce its efficiency.*

---

* Old alumni do not defend their schools out of mere sentimentality. Their own effectiveness in society depends on the preservation and constant regeneration of the networks of influence based in the schools.

Still more profoundly, the success of the *grandes écoles* answers certain fundamental needs in French society; the schools exist in symbiosis with the French social and bureaucratic system, which they reflect and whose stability they help to preserve. This extremely ponderous system would never have developed and survived without a stratum of leaders of high quality at its head. While the elite is ostensibly independent of the system and its constraints, it is, in fact, its necessary counterpart. Without it, the system would collapse, and without the system, the freedom and prestige of the elite would decline.

For a long time it was thought that only the higher managerial levels, freed from the constraints of day-to-day management, could dream up fresh solutions to social and technical problems, and that they alone had enough detachment and the requisite authority to impose solutions on the apparatus as a whole. But their style of success leads to routinization of executive and managerial jobs, imprisoning the managers themselves in an organization that soon becomes too passive to act. They find it harder and harder to impose their views, for the apparatus is no longer subject to their control. The protective gulf that surrounds the directorial elite ends by keeping its members in a constant state of frustration. Relations between those who conceive and those who execute become increasingly problematic, conflict-ridden, and rare. The lower and middle ranks participate in the general objectives of the organization only to a limited degree, and the most rational adjustment for them is to accept the routine imposed on them.

Worse still, this isolation of the elite is accompanied by fruitless rivalry between the various elite groups. At the top of the system, generalists no longer communicate with the engineers, and *polytechniciens* try to protect themselves from *énarques*. Communication is poor or nonexistent. The elite still rules, but over a desert. Chosen before it has gained any experience, incapable of real communication with colleagues and peers in rival groups, it rebels instinctively against any kind of intrusion from outside. It lives in a ghetto, and it becomes stale and impoverished.

Of course all this plays a vital part in the decline of French society's capacity for innovation. In the past, the *grandes écoles* system supplied French society with a considerable pool of intellectual talent. This manifested itself in the (admittedly painful) introduction of a great number of (not always competitive) innovations. But nowadays innovations can truly thrive only in a much broader intellectual environment—more diverse, rich, and open to all forms of contact. Not that creativity is passing out of the individual's hands into that of a team—as is all too often claimed—but because innovation requires a cooperative supporting environment in addition to individual creativity. The inability to create this environment has been a major reason for the failures and backwardness of the French intellectual world and, increasingly, French society as a whole.

The issues raised by the *grandes écoles* system finally boil down to two, it seems to me: first, their virtual monopoly on a certain number of functions—or, if one prefers, the rather too perfect correspondence between selection at entry and lifelong career prospects; second, the way the problem of hierarchy and compartmentalization arises among the schools and even within each one, tending to assign a role, philosophy, and territory to be defended to each section or subsection of the elite, so that each of these sections is unable to cooperate with the others and is ultimately unable to evolve and develop further.

The world of tomorrow will make it imperative that elites abandon their monopolistic traditions, open the door to individual competition and collective cooperation, and willingly accept the rise of people of lowly social origins. This can happen only if the French agree both to an increase in the number and diversity of each institution's "products" and to greater competition between them—which means that the hierarchies among them must disappear—so that a market can gradually develop that is sufficiently large, complex, and changing to prevent the re-emergence of these monopolies.

Liberal Revolution or Petit-Bourgeois Revolt?

French society overextended itself when it tried to modernize in accordance with its own traditions—that is, technocratically—and lost its nerve. The most natural reflex in this sort of situation is to back-pedal and to give up the effort to achieve rapid modernization. A positive response would be, rather, to blame the technocratic tradition itself, responsible as it is for the inability to carry out the necessary transformations. In the university, this would first and foremost mean liberalizing the system, both where it is too constraining and where it looked for the easy way out.

Since May 1968, two convergent pressures have tended to force the university back into its original state of impotence. The first is an obsessional retreat of large numbers of young people and intellectuals back to millenarian ideologies favoring total change; this has created a very strong force for blockage, in that much of the potential for change is thus spent in conservative action. The second is a natural temptation for governments and elites to buy social peace and isolation of the extremes at the expense of any structural change. It is possible to pacify the petite bourgeoisie with a series of bureaucratic protections that conform to socialist tradition as well as to the *étatique* and social Catholic traditions, thus temporarily calming the apprehensions of all groups threatened by change. In this context, the objective alliance between revolutionaries and conservatives must naturally make even the most generous reforms inoperable.

Attempts at innovation must therefore be of a totally different nature. Instead of trying to legislate for eternity by imposing the latest "best solution" or the most up-to-date, absolute, and ideal educational principles, we should aim simply to help systems that are now blocked in paralyzing stalemate situations to disengage from them. We can do this by mobilizing their own resources to the fullest extent.

To transform the *Polytechnique,* the *Ecole Centrale,* and the other main engineering schools into universities equal to the best technical universities in the world, to transform the *Ecole Nationale d'Administration* into a series of postgraduate programs in two or three good administration or management colleges, to replace drilling for the *grands concours* with tough but very open preparatory doctoral programs—such partial reforms may not seem very spectacular, but in the long run they would have a more powerful effect on the renewal of French society than the proclamation of any universal law.

The French university's bureaucracy has not succumbed beneath the shock of 1968. It has gradually weakened as it slowly adjusts to the most pressing demands, but it has rejected any suggestion of competition, it has maintained its monopolistic traditions, its inner divisions have become worse if anything, and it is still fearfully impotent. But the point is no longer to criticize, but rather to explore the institutional investments required for constructing (or rather reconstructing) living, creative university institutions. The best chances for success lie at the top of the system, in the transformation of those small, at present inaccessible, units constituting the *grandes écoles.* The process of breaking the stalemate France has reached in its educational system must begin with reform there.

CHAPTER SEVEN

The Meaning of the Crisis of May 1968

Crises are providential for the sociologist. They reveal the hidden truths of a social system better than anything else. All the most preposterous possibilities reappear, when they are usually out of the question in the normal course of events because of the constraints of the prevailing social game. Games break their rules, strategies are overthrown, behavior changes course, and the deepest and most secret control mechanisms finally have to be revealed.

It becomes a real temptation, unfortunately, to believe that crisis is truth, while the "regular" functioning of society is just a long nightmare. Many people cherish this illusion for a few weeks or months during a crisis; some militants who devote their lives to it find resources in this belief that religion no longer offers. But the analyst who yields to this temptation is like a psychiatrist who takes his patient's assertions at face value.

In the case of the May 1968 events in Paris, the problem was both simplified and complicated by the unusually dreamlike quality of the crisis. Between the waking dream, the dream spectacle, and the dream of a *société du spectacle,* the Parisian intellectual world for a time—a time that is still continuing for some—lost all sense of reality. And yet not one of the strands connecting the events to the fabric of everyday life in a modern consumer society was broken. The stopping of gas supplies, which occurred at the height of the spectacle, gave the drama a necessary unity of place, but that was all.

Every element of a traditional crisis occurred in 1968, yet the violence never went beyond what all Frenchmen implicitly understood to be the point of no return—physical death—and the government was not overthrown. It was quite astonishing, really, to observe this extreme proof of French society's sophistication: treating itself to a spectacle of its own deepest problems, wholly improvised, and yet sufficiently controlled to ensure that no irreparable harm was done.

But what could, and what can, an event that is nothing more than a spectacle signify? What could Frenchmen have meant to tell themselves by organizing this parody of the last two centuries of their history in the form of a contemporary "happening"?

It would seem at first sight that any interpretation is permissible, since nothing irreparable happened, since neither revolutionaries nor the defenders of order really fought with each other, since the king and his people parted without tears or blood and without knowing whether they ever really understood each other. But the hall of intellectual mirrors infinitely reflecting the dreams of this dream turns out to be very deceptive. No other event has shaken France's collective consciousness more profoundly, and we must analyze it more severely. The French, in manufacturing this psychodrama—or in yielding to it—were not asking that their exhibitions be taken at face value, but they did want their problems taken seriously.

Revolution Rediscovered or Undiscoverable Revolution?

The literal meaning of the May crisis was naturally a revolutionary one. The feelings and the passions it aroused, the mechanisms it set in motion, its unfolding and its logic were all revolutionary. All its characteristic acts had a precise significance in revolutionary symbolism. A barricade is a classic, almost ritual challenge. It was a question not of demonstrating, but of accomplishing symbolic acts with an insurrectional significance. It was unnecessary to occupy a building; all that was needed was to profane the authority exercised within that building. It was a question not of forcing teachers, employers, or managers to do or give something, but of humiliating, in them, the authority they were invested with.

It was therefore quite true that the ideology which best expressed the frenzied escalation of the "spirit of May" was that of its young *enragés* heroes. The fact that this ideology was heteroclite and contradictory mattered little; it fascinated Christians, non-Marxists, and the apolitical just as much as, possibly even more than, it did the Marxists themselves, not because of its content, but because it expressed the logic of the "movement" they were all caught up in. It was thus quite natural to interpret the events of May as the awakening of revolutionary enthusiasm, of a political fervor people had come to think of as moribund, and one did not have to go much further to see in 1968 the rumblings of popular anger, the tocsin of 1905, heralding a French October Revolution.

What lies beneath these symbols and this logic? Everyone involved, leaders of the movement as well as those who simply let themselves be carried along in the heat of the action, whatever their education or culture, thought basically in religious or even magical terms: the moment the sacred symbols of the Revolution appeared, revolutionary substance could not be far off; because the signs were there, the Revolution must be at hand.

Raymond Aron had little trouble in demonstrating the inconsistency and naïveté of this act of faith.* The message of May contained not the slightest revolutionary reality in the technical sense; no reasonable analyst could find any element of a proletarian revolution in the 1968 crisis. French society endured no process of disintegration. In Bolshevik terms,

* Raymond Aron, *The Elusive Revolution* (New York, 1969).

French workers are merely petit-bourgeois employees tainted by trade-unionist vice, and the French Communist Party bureaucracy, with all its caution and its Malthusian orthodoxy, adequately represents their prejudices and aspirations. This was amply demonstrated in real life: the students sought desperately to hand their revolution over to the people, who wanted nothing to do with it. Personalities and groups on all sides were eager to exploit the divine surprise of the events, but not a soul could be found to hold and cherish the revolutionary torch.

Aware of these difficulties, some of the May revolution's more sophisticated zealots, such as Alain Touraine,* have tried to get out of the impasse by transposing into the future this image of a revolution inherited from the past. Admitting that the students are not heralds of a proletarian revolution, he prefers to see them as actors in a new drama of class warfare between the proletariat and the technocrats of knowledge, a polarity that will be the underlying mainspring of post-industrial society in the same way that the struggle between capitalists and proletariat was the mainspring of industrial society.

It is a seductive idea, but its attractiveness is sentimental more than anything else. Why should university institutions dominate post-industrial society by modeling themselves on the capitalist factory? Is it not more reasonable to suppose that they will exercise real influence in society only if they show themselves able to devise a better model? What evidence is there to suggest that tomorrow's divisions will merely reproduce the mechanisms of the past? The divisions in the capitalist world did not reproduce the social and religious divisions of the feudal era. If the key to post-industrial society lies in knowledge, then we must expect other mechanisms of alliance and opposition than those formalized by Marx in his class-struggle scheme. The problems that Touraine deals with are certainly real problems, but by trying forcibly to apply the sacred symbolism of the revolutionary myth to them he fails to break with the magical reasoning that so profoundly united the students and intellectuals of May 1968.

* Alain Touraine, *Post Industrial Society* (New York, 1971).

Revolutionaries observed the existence of a revolutionary message and concluded that the revolution had arrived. Aron demonstrates that the revolution the May *enragés* were dreaming about cannot occur; he concludes that the message was therefore meaningless and that this "undiscoverable revolution" is no more than a reminiscence, a bad dream soon forgotten.

This skeptical reasoning may be just as valid against Touraine as it is against the classical revolutionaries, but I wonder whether its validity is not limited by the framework of the debate as it has been argued in France. This debate about the "meaning of May" got the French very excited, and even though it has become a dialogue of the deaf it still continues to agitate them, perhaps because it is one of those great escapist metaphysical contests that they love so much. It lets them forget reality.

Aron may well be right against the students, but he is not right where the events themselves are concerned. He is all too easily right when he faces opponents who are trapped in false logic. But the debate has gone too far off the rails for his refutation to work as a serious explanation of the events. It is true that May 1968 in France was not a revolutionary situation in the Marxist sense, but it is equally true to say that the crisis was profound, that it unfolded in a revolutionary manner, and that the message it delivered meant something. The fact that the Marxist, anti-Marxist, and para-Marxist quarrel is now outmoded does not mean that there is nothing left to look for. Quite the contrary.

May 1968 as the Expression
of the Stalemate Society

If we try to detach ourselves from the usual ideological vocabulary, from Marxist and anti-Marxist ways of reasoning, whose use tends, as we have seen, to obscure analysis, what is striking about the May crisis is that it was revolutionary neither in its political objectives nor in its social aims, but profoundly so in its means of expression—that is, where the mechanisms of the social process, or simply human relations, were concerned. The crisis produced neither a political nor a social breakdown, but it did produce cultural breakdown.

If this is so, we must develop an interpretation centered around the question of means rather than ends; we must look for the origins and mainspring of the crisis in the functioning of everyday institutions, not in the organization of French political or economic power. The French did not revolt in order to end capitalist exploitation or to build a classless society; they threw themselves into the crisis in order to attack a system of human relations, a style of action, a mode of management that was making them suffer.

The crisis of May 1968 thus appears as an attack upon the French style of action and as an instinctive revolt against what has been called the stalemate society.

In some ways the most characteristic features of the crisis may be seen as characteristics of the stalemate society. The stalemate society is founded on fear of face-to-face encounters and on a hierarchical conception of authority. So, let the crisis be a festival of face-to-face confrontations and challenges to authority!

In every sector, in every form of activity, and in every kind of group, customary human relationships were questioned. Intellectual activities were the most deeply affected, but no form of human action—from the schoolroom through factories, cooperatives, and religious communities to administrative offices—was spared this great wave of collective expression. Barriers and constraints gave way—or rather, with systematic zeal people sought to suppress all barriers to and constraints on communication. From a world of secrecy the French moved to a world of showdown. People who had been accustomed to protecting themselves from any kind of communication with each other drenched themselves in words. Secrets were made public, language taboos were violated, and people who never "had the time" to listen were forced to listen. At the same time, all forms of authority were challenged, and face-to-face encounters grew naturally out of these challenges, as if the deconsecration of authority and the commitment to a world of speech flowed ineluctably from the same rupture.

The compulsive, almost automatic nature of this upheaval was confirmed by a fact which perhaps not many people perceived very clearly but which was remarkable nonetheless. Very similar phenomena occurred everywhere in France, as if the initial symbolic breakdown at Nanterre and at the Sorbonne sounded a starting signal for an instinctive uprising by each social cell in turn, leading each one to adopt identical procedures and scenarios, despite the differences in situation, context, and issues at stake.

Still, the uprising was doomed to fail, could never have been anything but a world with no tomorrow, for no one broke with the system under attack. People automatically, almost stereotypically, could make speeches and attack authority because the question never arose of changing the system or the style, and there was consequently no need to seek any other means of resolving the inevitable conflicts between group and individual. People really thought they could break authority, as if it were a taboo, or take the floor, as if it were the Bastille. They did not look upon authority and communication in terms of their being human relations that are at once necessary and limited. It did not occur to them that a juxtaposition of liberated monologues can never form the basis of a community, or that the immediate, spontaneous relations of an unrestrained and leaderless crowd can never last longer than the space of a paroxysm.

Within their system, cut off from communication and human encounter, the French dreamed of total, spontaneous expression and communication. And within their system, they offered themselves a great carnival, where everything was possible precisely because it was a carnival. When they awoke, drunk and exhausted from the revelry, nothing had changed. Nothing in fact could have changed.

It is here that the problem takes on a new dimension. For this balancing out is no accident; it fits in with the logic of the stalemate-society system, of which instinctive revolt and temporary uprising are characteristic features.

As I have argued, the stalled society is based in effect on the constant opposition between always negative, always conservative groups and individuals (members of the group) who can exercise their personal creativity free from all responsibility thanks to the protection their membership affords them. Revolutionary as an individual, conservative as member of a group, the citizen of the stalled society wins both ways. But the institutions he belongs to would be doomed to immobility were it not for the occasional crisis that allows adjustments to be made. At these times, for a few brief moments during which the individual's creative impulses manage to break the group barriers, a new equilibrium emerges out of blind chaos. The results never live up to the hopes of the participants, and they are disproportionate to the energy expended. The fundamental characteristics of the system remain as they were before, but a certain number of problems do get resolved.

The phenomenon is particularly clear in the French political system. When a system is so perfectly integrated and rigid, as a result of its monolithic administrative apparatus, that there is nothing, other than certain protections, between the state and the citizen, it has considerable inertial force and can resist pressure over long periods through the sheer force of its blindness and deafness. But, once it is set in motion in a time of crisis, it becomes very difficult to stop. A few dozen students can, through an unexpected chain reaction, put the entire regime in jeopardy.

The events of May 1968 revealed both the rigidity and the fragility of the system. But at the same time they enabled us to appreciate what adjustments and corrections had been made by the bourgeois Third and Fourth Republics in the course of their long experiment, and how they had made the model more flexible. In particular, events showed that the old, fiercely criticized ministerial crises of the Fourth Republic used to act as a sort of automatic safety device that helped to avoid greater dangers. The typical Fourth Republic mini-crisis, with solutions hammered out in an atmosphere of urgency and confusion, was indispensable for the settlement of intractable problems away from the glare of publicity and compromise. The abolition in the Fifth Republic of this civilized, *ersatz* crisis merely helped to reinforce the general stalemate situation.

The acute crisis the Fifth Republic underwent in 1968 forced France to recognize these very deepseated tendencies, which were hard to discern in the course of the normal functioning of her institutions. The crisis threw light on them, but it did not create them, and we must conclude that if these mechanisms really are the fundamental ones of the stalled society, then the May crisis was not an attack on them but their clearest expression. What struck me most strongly in analyzing the events of May 1968 is the way they elucidated some of the most obscure phenomena in a society that is positively eager to conceal its most profound modes of regulation from itself. One is inclined to look upon it as an immense natural experiment, in which old hypotheses were put to the test and during which they were at least provisionally demonstrated.

Regression or Catharsis?

Our thinking on human relations and the mechanisms of social progress leads us to a level of discussion that goes far beyond a debate over revolutionary symbols. But the interpretation we arrive at must still remain partial.

The crisis of 1968 was an expression of the stalled society, and it also revealed this society's hidden tendencies and mechanisms. But did it in any way contribute to the evolution of this society? It conformed to the classical model. But was it nothing more than a reaffirmation of that model? Did it signal a return to tradition, or the beginnings of a break with tradition?

The first, most logical, and easiest interpretation is that this was a retrogressive crisis. The French-style bureaucratic system was threatened; changes taking place were beginning seriously to compromise its stability. The crisis, conforming perfectly to the classical model, was a step backwards. It re-established the fundamental equilibrium of a system that was beginning to find a new balance. It occurred not because French society was not changing, but because it was changing too fast. It was a crisis *within* the system enabling France to avoid a crisis *of* the system.

As I have tried to show, the French model is becoming increasingly inefficient in a world of accelerating change. It permits neither the minimum of communication nor the mobilization of human resources which are indispensable to the development of an industrial society. Its capacity for adaptation and innovation is severely limited. France's response to the modern world takes the form of highly technocratic (consequently maladroit) interventions by leaders in various sectors of activity, all of whom try to impose change from above, and always in the system's own style. Some modernization has been accomplished, but in an atmosphere of confusion and irresponsibility, and at the price of great tension. The authoritarian reformer, the only driving force in the system, has to make decisions blindly, imposing an unbearable material and affective cost on those he is continually pushing—against their will.

This leads to a climate of breakdown. We see this most clearly in the case of the university, with the Fouchet reform. But similar tensions also affected business, with executives' fears of reorganizations and mergers, and with growing fears of small shopkeepers and peasants about the stability of their environment. We could also see it in towns and cities, where the local notables spent their time resisting authoritarian attempts to reform financial and administrative structures. Even at the top, General de Gaulle's activism, and that of some of his ministers, served to weaken the state rather than strengthen it. The efforts made to change the aims, functions, and life style of the French were too hurried and too brutal, while at the same time they preserved the highly anachronistic form of government that was making change so unbearable.

The successful attempts at modernization and liberalization, however, increased criticism of the system and induced a desire for change. Everywhere the need to communicate and participate was asserted instinctively; forms of government to which people were materially opposed were attacked from an affective angle. The more rapid the change, the faster people lost faith in the virtues of the system, which appeared sooner or later to be doomed. It was as if, finally, French society had refused the jump, as if it had lost its nerve during an ill-conceived process of mutation that was nevertheless undermining the traditional ways of functioning.

However valid at a primary level of analysis, this interpretation does not allow us to conclude that the old mechanisms of French society had been reinforced. Of course the end of the 1968 crisis saw a great many restorations of the classical type and something of a relapse back into an enlarged and restabilized bureaucratic system; this was the case with the university. We might note, moreover, that the two most important crises in modern France before this one—in 1936 and following the Liberation in 1944—also led to an increase in bureaucratic rigidity, whatever their other effects. Still, one has the impression that the principal reaction among ruling circles on this occasion, unlike that in the other two crises, was a feeling of being overwhelmed rather than one of regressing. One may therefore ask whether this crisis, in bringing the old mechanisms to light, had not thereby largely devalued them, whether in the end it provoked an instinctive revulsion, and whether, in the last analysis, it did not act as a catharsis.

Let us go back to the image of the theatrical spectacle, for that, after all, is an ideal occasion for a "purging of passions."

The French dreamed aloud, and wide awake, of revolution; they dreamed they had finished the job when really they had done nothing of the kind; and finally a strong consensus emerged among the protesters themselves* in favor of keeping the agitation this side of farce and rowdyism—these seem to me to be some of the decisive features of the May 1968 events.

---

* Except among a small minority, whose influence was limited by its sectarianism.

French society was challenged deeply. It went as far as it could—but not to *do* anything, only to look. It *almost* exploded, *almost* carried out a total revolution. But it was really playing a game, experimenting. And there is another meaning expressed in this "almost," this experimenting. We showed ourselves our own feelings, our own possibilities, and our limitations. We pushed things to absurd lengths, playing the game to the point of paroxysm and seeking for effects. But this, of course, is the essence of theater and of the fascination it always exercises in developed societies. Why should we not conclude that, as in the theater, a profoundly cathartic function was being fulfilled here?

Perhaps experience will show that the generation which created May 1968 was the first to break with France's traditional attachment to revolutionary illusions, the absurdity of which it was better able to appreciate than preceding generations. Perhaps it acted out and parodied the history books because it was just about ready to close them. De Gaulle had insisted on playing Richelieu and Louis XIV. The *enragés* of May 1968 answered by acting out the great scenes of 1793 and 1848. But once the General died and the show was really over, one may well ask whether his ten years of *son et lumière,* culminating in the apotheosis of May 1968, did not function principally as a sort of exorcism. Perhaps later we shall say that a great change in French customs and manners dates from this period.

Certainly the political desert in the post-Gaullist period, the bleakness of public opinion, and the disarray of traditional thinking (emphasized but also exaggerated by commentators) do not amount to progress. But at least these reactions enable France to bring new life to the mechanisms of her traditional processes. Already there is a perceptible change in sensibility, and perhaps it is this which is causing anxiety and unease. Bureaucrats of the state and captains of industry are beginning to see how ridiculous it is to boast of their pretentious and muddleheaded activities, which do little more than stifle serious initiatives (which always come from below). Mandarins of every stripe are now more scrupulous in making decisions. A process of liberalization is once more beginning to spread through French society. Of course the future is never certain and the game has yet to be won, but perhaps now there is a real chance that French society will open up.

In these circumstances, the French elites are going to bear a heavy responsibility, and it is one for which they are ill prepared. The ultimate significance of the strange crisis that gripped all France in 1968, but that was aimed principally at them, will depend in effect upon their conscious choices and their unconscious behavior in the years to come. If they once again seek to protect themselves from all forms of criticism, and to preserve their privileges at all costs, then France will have given in, once more, to her old demons and will be shut forever in the closed and unending circuit of protest between irresponsible radicalism and the corporate demands of bureaucrats and petite bourgeoisie. If they opt for liberalization and evolution, the May crisis will come to be seen as the last great fling which this old, incurably romantic nation had to indulge in before entering the responsible world.

PART THREE
TOWARD A STRATEGY OF CHANGE

CHAPTER EIGHT

Renewal of the Intellectual Method

From an intellectual, moral, and political point of view, the crisis of May 1968 marked for France the end of an era and the coming of a new sensibility.

But if the crisis was most serious in France and for that reason more easily distinguishable there—if not analyzable—the change occurred everywhere and did not even start in France. The French crisis took on a very special meaning concerning the country's system of government and style of action, but it was part of a more general movement, a sort of upheaval that occurred at the end of the 1960s throughout the civilized world.

Something is dead which was once hope and which now seems to have been illusion—a certain oversimple rationalism, a facile confidence in reason, convergence, and progress—and its disappearance leaves us helpless. This change, like the breakdown in France, has brought on a raging ideological fever. But, again as in the May 1968 crisis, what it attacks are modes of thought and the governmental systems supporting them, rather than moral principles.

To understand this crucial problem, I can think of no more revealing, spectacular, and probing example of the change in sensibility than that concerning the cold war and the rivalry between the superpowers.

The End of the Dream of Convergence

Who would have thought, twenty years ago, that the hope of a convergence between the American and Soviet systems—a hope then so bold that only a few advanced thinkers dared formulate it during the long night of the cold war—was to become, for protesters in the late 1960s and a good proportion of the younger members of the intellectual elite they influenced, a hateful reality in a corrupt, oppressive world? Who would have thought it even a decade ago, when we were still fired by those great apostles of tolerance and liberalization, Kennedy, Khrushchev, and Pope John XXIII? But this spectacular reversal is only one of many that have characterized the years of moral and intellectual crisis we have lived through. The dream of convergence collapsed together with the ideal of progress, a certain facile and ill-defined confidence in human reason and liberal faith (of which the Peace Corps was one of the best expressions, but of which we can also find traces in Khrushchev's exuberance and Pope John's simplicity).

What was the basis for this talk of coexistence? Its logic was founded on an implicit gamble. Since ideological fanaticism, expressed in two different conceptions of the world, seems to be at the source of the opposition, we must try to seek in an understanding of the underlying sociological reality the true reasons for hope and the possibilities for further development.

If only we could manage to shift the field of discussion, we used to think, then the Russians and Americans would discover that their problems and the constraints upon them were basically the same. Both depend on large organizations, and both have to accept the constraints imposed by this. They are subject to the same routines and complications, and they enjoy the same advantages of security and relative equality. They have to accord increasing importance to experts of all kinds, without whom the extraordinarily complex machinery they have evolved could not function. They must devote ever greater efforts to scientific research, and they must respect the freedom of scientists, who have also become indispensable. Finally, they are dominated at all levels by managers, who are concerned more with efficiency than with ideals.

At the same time, it was thought, recognition of these problems and constraints should lead not only Russia and the United States but all modern societies to hasten the natural process of evolution toward convergence. By progressing from an economy of scarcity to one of abundance, the Russians would be obliged to relax and decentralize their economic system; they would be forced to reintroduce the market system and, by consequence, to liberalize their political system. The Americans, for their part, would be increasingly forced to intervene in their economy in order to maintain growth; regulation of the economic and social spheres would necessarily become more conscious and more responsible. Scientific investment, which determines the pace and direction of overall technological development, would increasingly be coordinated and carried out by the state. The multitude of transfer payments would emphasize the regulated, if not planned, character of economic life. There was little difference—and there would be even less—between a society dominated by large, privately owned organizations that are increasingly planned, and a society dominated by large public organizations which, out of a desire for efficiency, are trying to foster flexibility and adaptability and to mobilize the personal initiative characteristic of the market economy.

Even the Catholic Church's *aggiornamento*, in its efforts to keep pace with the modern world and to adopt a new, more human face, could be seen as an effort in the same direction. Teilhard de Chardin's philosophy of "general ascension" was especially well suited to this purpose.

Only a few years later, both East and West seem to have abandoned these enthusiasms in favor of the old skepticism; all that remains is an aftertaste of failure. Not only does coexistence, pursued with so much fervor a decade ago, no longer interest us, but we have lost interest in taking chances or in conquest; we now seek only to bear witness. A cycle of absurdity and derision has begun once more to haunt our unconscious, the more violently and the more desperately since we lowered our ancient barriers and precautions when we enjoyed that climate of hope.

What forced our hopes off the rails? The severity of the setback is such that we cannot account for it merely by the chance occurrence of historical events. We must look deeper than that. And analysis of the change may help us to understand the logic of the systems it brought down; and it ought therefore to lead us to investigate more seriously the intellectual method we use in conceiving and governing our future.

Of course the objectives themselves were not misconceived. Who could object to the idea of peaceful coexistence internationally, or to the rejuvenation of national institutions? But were these realistic aims? Had we reasonably assessed the data on which we claimed to be working? And was there any real justification for the intellectual method we based our actions on?

First of all, we either forgot or deliberately ignored the immense superiority of the American system—not in terms of present wealth so much as in terms of its capacity for further development. Certainly the cold-war balance of nuclear terror was perfectly symmetrical, but it was a static, military symmetry; the prevailing conditions called for two equal players, regardless of wealth and power, placing their own lives at stake. All men are equal in the face of death, but not in the face of life. The differences between America and Russia become more noticeable when we look at the civil performance of the two systems.

We can call the ruling strata of both countries "technostructures," and this will emphasize that they play similar roles in their respective systems. But this logical symmetry should not hide the fact that the American technostructure can mobilize a far greater wealth of resources, can act more flexibly and effectively, and possesses a far greater general capacity for innovation. This difference is even more marked now that global détente is increasing it. The cold war, with its restrictions and barriers, protected the more rigid Russian system, concealing its failings and paralyzing its opponent. Relaxation of international tension, on the other hand, is advantageous to the more flexible system. The convergence theory, which sought to place the two systems on an equal footing, merely increased the Soviet handicap. Paradoxically, it was in the cold-war confrontation that the two systems resembled each other most closely, while the lowering of tension and liberalization enabled the more powerful to benefit from a reinforcement of its particular characteristics.

In the short term at least, contrary to what was once believed, international relaxation has not encouraged convergence. Instead, it has favored the system best adapted to competition, the only possible convergence thus being an American convergence. The ideal of convergence, originally a pacifist ideal, thus inevitably became a potentially dangerous source of instability.

Second, we forgot or refused to assess correctly the very great organizational differences between American corporations— American organizations in general—and those in the USSR. The fact that the problems are similar does not mean there is only one answer to them. "Managers" do indeed share certain characteristics in all countries, but their modes of thinking and styles of action differ greatly from one country to another. The growth of "planning" in American big business should mislead no one into thinking this resembles Soviet planning. The general trend in the United States is not toward a routinization of producer-customer relations (although in certain branches of industry we do find evidence of a conditioning of demand, as Galbraith has described) but, rather, toward more rational strategies that entail calculated risks but do not involve commitment to an exclusive relationship. The monopolistic spirit seems to be diminishing with the scientific explosion, thus drawing the pattern of American business even further away from the Soviet one, which has been unable to free itself despite desperate governmental efforts.

It is only where the *social* consequences of development are concerned that planning regains the utility it has lost in the economic sphere. The convergence we were hoping for does not seem to be occurring in business—we are perhaps more likely to find it in the somewhat symmetrical efforts both nations are now making to remedy very different problems—and instead of being a force for change or renewal, the dream of convergence is now becoming a brake on both the Western and the Soviet systems, an excuse, a facile alibi for preserving the status quo. The younger generation's revolt against organizational constraints may be ill directed and may have failed to comprehend the real conditions of human freedom. But it was the natural result of the static vision within which the liberal dream of progress trapped us. Instead of its becoming aware of the problems raised and potentials made available in society's rational, ever more complex, and changing activities, it got the impression that we had entered an era of stability and conformism.

Finally and most important, we profoundly underestimated one last source of instability—the acceleration of scientific development. We tended to reason as if we had mastered the consequences of development, and as if modern economic theory could erase the most brutal changes and breakdowns while maintaining stable growth.

But the harmony of aggregate national curves should not blind us to local crises and transformations. Economic growth is continuing, and the increasingly rapid transformation of scientific discoveries into technological advances will only widen the disparities and divergences between nations, regions, social categories, and sectors. Development obeys linear extrapolations from the statistical curves only in the short term. Although these constitute our best approximations of the overall situation, they give us a very poor idea of real-life conditions. The harmonious growth observed in the aggregate hides a multitude of crises of change and regression. Moreover, the theory which concluded that, since we knew the principal characteristics of development, we could now fully plan our economies, was an overhasty one. We are not entering a finite world. On the contrary, the range of possibilities is widening. Liberalization is encouraging this process, and this once more works in favor of the American system.

The immensity of the human destiny opening up before us cannot be welcomed as an unmixed blessing. It is not because it resoundingly refutes both right-wing and left-wing conservative philosophers predicting the end of freedom that modern societies can look to the future with confidence; quite the reverse. The responsibilities implied by the discovery of so much potential for freedom are awesome, and they are a source of anxiety that modern man is finding it harder and harder to master.

This is why, despite appearances, it is on the human level that American society is now most vulnerable. Not because it is oppressive, but because it changes faster and because it is further advanced in the process of cultural change. It can even be said to be the victim of the democratic mechanisms that have fostered its extraordinary material success. Being far more involved in the collective adventure than citizens of more stratified societies, Americans are forced to internalize all their social conflicts and contradictions far more thoroughly than members of societies where responsibility for change can be thrust upon the leaders or upon a more coercive system.

The Collapse of the Liberal Synthesis

Contrary to our earlier and premature hopes for convergence in the short and medium term, for harmony governed by rational, liberal, or collectivist progress, the modern world is more likely to be one of breakdown, of divergences and disparities between nations, systems, and groups. If this is so, we may be justified in thinking that what is really at stake in this great unanticipated test of active coexistence is not long outworn ideologies but the intellectual methods used in conceiving and organizing collective action.

Soviet-style planning-oriented rationalism was the first to be hit. It could maintain the illusion of efficacy only in an atmosphere of constraint and secrecy. Once the field of international competition widened beyond military affairs to consumer goods, its ineffectiveness became obvious.

This is not an issue of ideals or objectives; everyone in all industrialized nations has long agreed that the main priorities are to increase production and to ensure that this production satisfies man's basic needs, that wastage is deplorable and unemployment evil, that it is better to organize human activities rationally than to let the law of the jungle take over. The heart of the matter is an issue of means, and the methods that enable us to use them. Now it so happens that in the Soviet system the weight and the cost of the means are insupportable. They make communication between the base and the summit extremely difficult, they falsify information, they inhibit the many and rapid adjustments required by the changing environment, they discourage innovation and stifle potential human resources. The synthetic, deductive, *a priori* method justifying the use of these means is rigid and makes it hard to learn by experience. In fact, the Soviet leaders prefer major periodic administrative revolutions, while in the meantime borrowing American techniques, procedures, and even solutions in order to rethink the principles and methods of action that are the real cause of their failures.

Oddly, the totalitarian weakness of the administrative machine offers rather effective protection for the regime's intellectuals. Its successive failures in economic and social affairs act to strengthen the need for constraint—the very cause of the most deepseated blockages—thus protecting the system's engineers and ideologists and their rationalist clear conscience from serious criticism.

For some years the failures of Soviet planning seemed to offer a sure justification for the claims of American liberal intellectuals. The liberal synthesis they inspired seemed in contrast the final (and only) possible incarnation of reason. But their success bore within it the seeds of ruin, and it was because of this success, not in spite of it, that the liberal synthesis found itself ever more directly and harshly challenged than Soviet rationalism was.

In 1960 it seemed different. The electoral defeat of populist and anti-intellectual elements rang in an era of liberalism triumphant. The resounding humiliation of Russia at the time of the Cuban missile crisis was a crowning success for the new modes and methods of reasoning. Its demonstration of America's superior capacity for development, organization, change, and action in general (which was becoming evident in most branches of human activity) seemed ultimately to be the consequence of its superior intellectual method rather than of its material and financial resources.

But these successes were dangerous in themselves. For as long as power had been held by conservatives or moderates, the liberal synthesis had been protected by a barrier of traditions and prejudices, but when its advocates came to power, they came face to face with their responsibilities, and their weaknesses were revealed—both in foreign policy, dominated by an absurd colonial war they could neither foresee nor stop nor understand, and at home, where the racial explosion came at the very moment when, from the liberal viewpoint, progress had been greatest.

In order to understand this spectacular and quite unexpected failure, we must analyze the logic of liberalism, a logic first and foremost based on certain principles. Undoubtedly, these principles are more complex and more sophisticated than those of Soviet rationalism, but they are beginning to look threadbare nonetheless. The best proof of this lies in the fact that no one now dares object to them. Who would be so bold as to claim he was *not* rational, progressive, moral, democratic, universalist? This unanimity is a weakness rather than a strength, a sign that the intellectual debate has moved to another level and that it is no longer possible to deduce a model of action from these principles.

In fact, the true characteristic of the liberals was not fidelity to principles that are now useless because they were too successful, but a certain decisive and peremptory manner of putting them into effect. Their great weakness lay in their belief that time would stand still and that it was possible to transform their principles into a rational synthesis that would let them have an answer for everything. In the event, this consisted in extrapolating from the trends, data, and knowledge of the contemporary American experience to all American society and, ultimately, to the whole world. All elites have yielded to this sin of pride and self-sufficiency, but the acceleration of the pace of history precipitated this, punishing the sinners at the very moment when their own success was generating a new dynamic they could not control.

And in order to preserve the universal model that had once enabled them to tie up all the elements of their synthesis coherently, American liberals were driven to suppress contradictions, deform reality, and, finally, exhaust their intellectual resources with the same recklessness those in power showed in attempting to preserve the global *pax Americana.* There is a certain justice in the fact that the current wave of apocalyptic protest has selected these liberals as its main target. However absurd the protest may be, it is playing a vital role in the criticism of a method and logic that are no longer capable of self-renewal.

The gradual ruin of the liberal edifice was finally brought on by the tragedy of Vietnam. But this accident of fate merely served to precipitate events. The very visible exhaustion of the archetypal liberal is more profound. One had the feeling, with the defeat of Hubert Humphrey,* that an era was drawing to a close.

French society never experienced the splendors of liberalism triumphant. The success of the republican-socialist synthesis, which echoed it, was only partial and temporary. But the same wear and tear seem to have affected the socialist, radical,

---

* George McGovern's campaign shifted away from the model only very partially.

"federalist," and centrist currents within that synthesis. Their divisions and repeated failures saved French "liberals" from exercising overburdensome responsibilities, but the exhaustion of all their forces for renewal, which they never managed to mobilize, seems to be general. The intellectual weariness of the Mendès-France–Defferre team in the 1969 French presidential elections was just as obvious as Humphrey's and seems sufficient to explain its defeat.

Toward a New Intellectual Method

Ultimately we shall find that the best opportunity for renewal lies at the level of intellectual methods; but we shall also find there the heaviest responsibilities. The present crisis has seriously weakened the parties for change in Western societies and, with them, one of the essential elements of our philosophy of action. It strikes very deep, for the preservation and survival of our societies depends upon their dynamism.

I think it is quite mistaken to respond to this crisis by questioning the objectives, the ideology, or the moral principles upon which this philosophy was founded. The real problem is the underlying type of action and intellectual method. This is what makes it so hard for society to confront the problem, at least at the start. Since we cannot perceive the sources of the trouble we feel, and since we cannot really attack the principles or advance serious ideological alternatives, the will to renewal tends to become rebellion without a cause.

If we take the case of the United States, responsibility for the collapse of the liberal synthesis should be sought in the two (opposing) methods upon which it was founded: incrementalism and global policy planning.

Incrementalism may be defined as the method that consists in considering collective action solely in terms of the problems posed by the mutual adjustment of all the actors involved. In this model, no reasonable action can be carried on if it is based on an *a priori* synthesis. In the American case, it basically rationalizes the mutual-adjustment practices that are the hall-mark of American-style pluralist democracy, and it extends liberal economic philosophy to the entire range of public collective activities. In economics, one thus demonstrates that, in a given market, the sum of all the micro-adjustments of all the parts give better results than any form of *a priori* planning or coordination. And therefore in politics too one is supposed to abandon "policy" in favor of calculating the marginal costs and benefits of each possible approach to a problem and as a function of the pressures exercised by the parties involved.*

The incremental rule of action assumes the existence of a perfectly neutral and rational universe, without any particular bond, dependency, or viscosity. It can be invoked as an ideal somewhat in the same sense as one can invoke the withering away of the state: it would be a great advance if all the players in the social game could be perfectly neutral and rational, and we should make every effort to try to advance in this direction. But this bears absolutely no relation to reality, since we discover relations of dependence and knots of power distorting our progress at all the levels at which action occurs, and while progress seems possible, it is hard to eliminate these obstacles entirely. In the present Western context, incrementalism often leads to results that wholly negate the original liberal objective, whether in the sort of blind escalation of which Vietnam is just one example or, more often, in the development of vicious circles of poverty, economic stagnation, and cultural and social regression. While incrementalism has never been presented as a conscious political method in Europe, it forms in fact—just as much as in the United States, and with perhaps even more undesirable consequences—the basis of practical political action there too.

Global policy planning, coherent action plans, are of course intellectually more satisfying. Around them, a synthesis or successive syntheses are formed. But there is always a deep

---

* This method is best formulated by Charles Lindblom in *The Intelligence of Democracy* (New York, 1965).

contradiction between the desire for globalism that inspires these plans and the practice of incrementalism upon which they must depend. Even more important, the natural consequence of the very complex *a priori* reasoning they presuppose is that they are usually based on superficial knowledge and hasty extrapolations, their only unifying quality being a highly arbitrary need for coherence. It is at this global level that the artificial pattern of convergence, which has only served to exacerbate international conflict, has been played out and lost.

But to transcend this opposition between incrementalism and globalism we have to reject it and go beyond both, we have to analyze the real regulations of the multiple systems upon which we must act, and upon which we can only act incrementally.* The intellectual method we are fumbling for is one that will enable us to discover the key points of these systems, so that we can concentrate the free resources of society—or at least those autonomous sectors capable of action—on these points. Our resources, which are always inadequate, should be applied only at those points where they can be most effective. It is not a matter of substituting a piece or element of public power for the system already in operation, or of adding a new system alongside the old, but of contributing to the planned action by changing its rules so that new processes can give different results.

This method should also allow us to launch and encourage institutional—or more generally collective—learning processes analogous to those we can already set in motion at an individual level. The multiple systems that make up our basic units of collective action consist of men who individually are capable of learning, but whose collective actions seem immune to conscious and rational intervention. To transform this pattern of action constitutes the only acceptable kind of progress within

---

* The temporary and relative success enjoyed by French planning is mostly due to the fact that it was only a partial, abstract, artificial model imposed on economic and social reality. Behind its unwarranted ambitions, it effected a modest and reasonable combination of the incrementalism of its "planning parties" and the globalism of views advanced at the top.

the context of democracy—which, appearances notwithstanding, no one has ever thought of questioning.

But can we make this advance? Yes, certainly. We still know very little about how most systems are regulated, even about their existence. We do not as yet have the intellectual capacity to analyze the even larger groups in which we must act, which are systems of systems. But a number of experimental systems analyses have shown that one can go beyond incrementalism and become more operational, and this is encouraging.

Let us take the simplest example, that of an underdeveloped region or sector of an economy. The problem is not in itself one either of pricing (or the price of raw materials) or of investment. It is both of these, or much more (or perhaps less), according to the case in question—but not in the usual way. It is a systems problem. At the root of the economic stagnation we are trying to remedy we invariably find one or several vicious circles of *human relations,* in which the unfavorable results obtained collectively by the actors only serve to reinforce the behavior which is the cause of their poor cooperation in the first place. Any systemic functioning involves a certain amount of circularity, but when this exceeds a certain critical point the human group affected by it finds itself stuck in a process of cumulative stagnation or regression—and it is this which appears as a sign of comparative underdevelopment.

Means applied directly to such processes have only a very uncertain effect. Thus, there is no point in developing education if the absence of jobs leads naturally to a flight of the best people, who leave behind an absence of initiative that further hampers the creation of jobs. If one tries to remedy each of these elements of the problem, one will quickly find oneself involved in an enormous undertaking of prohibitive cost and dubious advantage, since experience shows that welfare dependency leads to still further vicious circles of dependence and impotence. Principles of equality of treatment or rational improvement, whether socialist revolutionary or managerial, are not of the slightest use at this level. On the other hand, we know that to give the automatic adaptive mechanisms free play would simply lead to continued stagnation, or even to eventual regression, and the human consequences then would be scandalous.

So the problem is to find a mode of responsible action somewhere between a global policy, which affects reality only through very costly and inefficient bureaucratic action, and incremental intervention based on *laissez faire,* which does not let one alter the balance of inequalities or waste that preserve injustice and stifle most people's creative possibilities. This first implies the need to discover the "knots" of power, of dependence, more generally of asymmetrical relations in the human group in question. The point of equilibrium must also be found, as well as opportunities for encouraging evolution. Two types of knowledge help us to define a strategy: knowledge of the types of regulation that govern these human relations (or rather, the system of which they are the expression), and knowledge of the types of learning process suited to the human groups or subgroups in question. It is not easy to acquire this knowledge, and we are still a long way from possessing the needed range of experience and theory, especially where collective learning is concerned. But we can say that skillful use of our present analytical capacity should, in a great many cases, enable us to determine the most sensitive points of the system whose evolution we wish to further. It should also enable us to bring about, at the least cost, the changes needed to stimulate the learning processes that constitute the only solution to the problem. It is clear that many major development programs launched in the past have had very little effect, and many actions undertaken by public authorities or other agents upon whom we can act easily—actions concerning, for example, the regulation of certain basic activities, the creation of an environment favorable to innovation, or the encouragement of certain people or groups to take certain risks—have been organized in such a way that they worked exactly counter to the intended objectives. By reorienting these efforts, we could obtain far more positive long-term results at modest cost. We are now beginning to realize that this kind of thinking is absolutely vital where urban problems and problems of poverty are concerned. More generally, in all major issues of cultural development, of underprivileged minorities, or even of education, we must stop thinking in terms of principles and undertake instead an analysis of the systems through which, and the processes whereby, our activities can be carried on and transformed.

Only in this perspective can the parties for change hope to renew themselves—whether in Europe or in the United States. If they refuse this "professional retraining," they will never escape the systems that now keep them trapped. They will discover the road to more limited, but more direct, responsibility that lies between the arrogance of macro-decisions and the blindness of micro-decisions, only if they abandon their narrow rationalism.

This method does not permit us to escape the logic of the opposing East-West systems or the need to re-examine our final goals, not to mention their underlying principles and ideologies. But at least it has the merit of offering a more neutral perspective, one that depends less on the general objectives and the practical constraints set by the logic of the large systems. It assumes no *a priori* convergence and commits nothing irrevocably in that direction. It can thus become a factor for general development—separate from ideologies and untouched by the ideology of convergence.

CHAPTER NINE

Problems and Priorities

To plan the future, to plan development, to make conscious decisions about the future of society—that is to say, our future and our children's future—is the most noble task of all. Everyone agrees with this, just as everyone agrees with democracy. But the ordinary citizen is ill at ease when faced with the ramifications of this idea as they might be incarnated in the policies of his country. Planning activity naturally arouses two contradictory reactions (both vitally important, for they ultimately determine the overall direction our policies take): panic in the face of the complexity and the constraints of modern life, leading the citizen to demand guarantees and protection; and a presumption that the human race pursues relatively simple goals in the main, and that all we have to do is to agree on them and set up priorities.

These two pressures determine the underlying significance of practical policies intended to protect the citizen from evolution, while claiming to control it in the name of an ideal no one can agree on. If we are to escape from this contradiction, we must first understand the logic of development our leaders claim to be acting upon.

We must not be satisfied, as we have too often been in the past, with an analysis of economic development that makes economics subservient to a philosophical ideal. Philosophical ideals, like economics, should be seen in the context of a far broader and ultimately more specific evolution—that of human relationships.

We generally look on modern man as burdened with a whole range of servitudes. All around us bureaucracies threaten us, superhighways push us around, leisure becomes a mass commodity, and thought itself is manipulated.

These are illusions, of course. This assertion may come as something of a surprise in an intellectual world dominated by fantasies of conditioning and manipulation. But if we could make a serious time-comparison—a sort of examination of the consciousness of the human race—we would find that the two most marked tendencies in all human activity are toward freedom (men are increasingly free to choose from among an ever greater number of possibilities) and toward calculation (they are constantly obliged to forecast the results of their actions and to calculate their cost).

The essential characteristic of modern society is the multiplication of material and spiritual exchanges between men. We can see this clearly when we analyze the fascination exercised by large cities. It is all very well to dream of the "country life," but if we prefer the city it is because of the extraordinary wealth of contacts and stimulation it offers. But why should this wealth automatically be a sign of great freedom?

In order to understand this, compare the behavior of a man born into a rural village before the industrial era with that of a man living in a large city, the best image of the post-industrial society of tomorrow. As a member of a small community, the villager was shut within a closed network of relations. Of course he was free to leave his village, but only at very great material and emotional cost, and he almost certainly finished up in another village similar to his own.

We frequently fail to perceive the consequences of this state of affairs. Man in village society is deprived of choice not merely because there are only a few human beings with whom he is likely to have the chance to associate, but because the impossibility of changing partners prevents him from taking any risk in the relationships to which he is committed. He can learn only with very great difficulty, because he is incapable of elucidating experience. He is thus condemned to resignation and repression, as a result of which his human experience is limited.

This is still a common situation for much of the population of even the most advanced societies—in geographical, professional, social, or even racial blocs characterized by an impoverished system of relations. These isolated communities pose a major obstacle to development.

As opposed to this, metropolitan man has a far wider range of choice, one which in the future at least is virtually unlimited. More important, he enjoys greater freedom in each of the relationships he chooses. In addition to this freedom to choose a job, a spouse, friends, all of which we might term first-degree freedoms, he has a second-degree freedom, which consists in being able to express himself with fewer inhibitions and with less fear in each of his relationships. And we can begin now to glimpse the spread of a third-degree freedom, in people's readiness to experiment and to innovate and in their capacity to transcend social determinisms.

These freedoms differ totally from past conceptions of freedom. In a society in which exchanges were limited, hence exacting and hence dangerous, the individual was tempted to seek his freedom in isolation and independence from others. In a society where exchanges are richer and freer, they become less threatening, and man learns to find his freedom in a multiplicity of relationships and contacts. The greater the variety of relationships he has, the less he risks becoming dependent.

Rational calculation and measurement—to come to the second major tendency—permit human activities to be regulated by sanctions depending on results, rather than by means that restrict freedom (such as hierarchical constraints, ideological pressure, manipulated information).

But, in spite of appearances, it seems to be extremely difficult for modern man to make this transformation to rational calculation, since it cannot be effected from above like an imposed constraint. It can develop only through the conversion of the individual who is to be its object, who must learn for himself how to calculate rationally, with and against the collective activities in which he participates. This learning process is possible only if freedom of choice grows at the same time; it has long been paralyzed by our leaders' reluctance to allow it to develop.

The Problems of the Individual

This vision of the future is not an idyllic one, as my foreshortened treatment of it may suggest. There are still the numberless inconveniences to which modern man is subject, and the extremely high price he has to pay for his freedom.

The point is not to complain or to denounce, but to understand. If our problems are difficult ones, this is because it is very difficult to take on the kind of freedom associated with rational calculation.

We generally stand things on their heads, and we assume that man has a natural passion for freedom and that it is the oppressiveness or the conditioning of society that prevents him from achieving it. In fact, however, we all fear freedom—other people's freedom (since this introduces uncontrollable variables into our personal arrangements) and our own (which represents the most anxiety-producing of all risks).

In the still-traditional society of the nineteenth century, individuals were protected by barriers of class, caste, and education that enormously restricted competition. In most cases individual careers and fates were pursued within closed markets. Of course there were opportunities for adventurers, but mostly the factors of determinism, origins, nepotism, et cetera, predominated. Today, to the degree that privileges are weakening or disappearing, barriers are falling, and obstacles to freedom of choice are breaking down, competition is becoming much fiercer, and individuals are losing a good deal of their security. True, they are given impersonal guarantees in return which offer sometimes much greater material security. But these guarantees have very little effect on their psychological security and on their self-awareness. They will certainly not resolve or alleviate the identity crisis provoked by the increase in freedom —that is to say, by the increase in uncertainty.

If, on the other hand, the multiplicity of exchanges possible today enriches people, leading them to a higher stage of development, it also requires a difficult learning process, and this generates very fierce tensions. In a traditional society made up of groups cut off from one another, where exchanges are few and difficult, each individual identifies with his primary group, adopting its quarrels and conflicts without question. In a society where exchanges are multifarious, one person will belong to a great variety of networks and systems of relations, some of them with conflicting interests and viewpoints. This does not mean that the conflicts are attenuated, but it does mean that the individual is obliged in part to internalize them. Society today contains a far greater number of positions implying conflicting loyalties. Even those people whose role is fairly simple or isolated are continually divided among opposing points of view; this certainly enables them to escape the determinisms of a closed environment, whose features converge, but it also forces them into incoherence, contradiction, and the anguish of choice.

In short, the growth of rationality, obliging every individual to calculate an ever-growing number of elements of his behavior, cannot but transform our lives. In some ways it is easier to obey someone else and settle down as a spectator than to have the duty, in a free society, to look upon oneself as the instrument of one's own calculations.

Though the constraints are of a different order, being no longer ones that men exercise over other men but ones that individuals exercise over themselves, the number of constraints is effectively greater than before, and people need far greater human resources to cope with them. The learning process to which we are constantly condemned has nothing to do with the standardization we are always warned about. On the contrary, it ought to be viewed as an enrichment, but it does involve a very difficult psychological mutation.

When a person runs out of excuses and alibis, the problem of the risks of failure—and of having to explain away one's failures—becomes much more disturbing, if not unbearable.

New Collective Capacities

The problem assumes the dimensions of a crisis of civilization, insofar as the irresistible pressure for individual freedom of choice is undermining traditional social taboos (such as sexual taboos), while the development of rational calculation is revealing the need for new controls. The greater our awareness of the consequences of our acts, the stronger the pressure becomes to eliminate the risks they entail—and this is so whether we are talking about health, education, welfare, pollution, or even cultural and racial issues. But it is at this point precisely that we lack the traditional principles in whose name it was formerly possible to control the activities of our fellow men. There is only one way out of this dilemma: the formation of human groups able to withstand the most powerful tensions and contradictions.

My formulation may appear tautological. But, on closer inspection, human groups have always had to cope with contradictory demands in order to govern themselves: rights of the individual versus the needs of the group, need for constraint and security versus the need for motivation and participation, stability versus innovation, and so on. What the organizations and systems to which we belong now require is a new capacity enabling us consciously to face up to more direct and much clearer contradictions.

This organizational capacity does not exist naturally; it is a human conquest, the fruit of a long learning process. But once it is acquired, man can become freer and better able to support the consequences of newly clear choices and precisely measured results. To this organizational capacity we should add a "systemic" capacity, consisting in the ability to develop and observe rules, customs, systems of human relations, and processes of social control, without which a society is incapable of bringing its problems to light and dealing with them. These organizational and systemic capacities, I repeat, are not the consequences of development but its first and most essential condition. A society can advance, can tolerate greater freedom and clarity in human commitments insofar as it develops the organizational or systemic capacity to deal with these changes.

France in Evolution

All societies, even the most advanced ones, have great difficulty in dealing with the problems posed by this evolution toward greater freedom and rationality in human relations. But traditional blockages place French society in an especially critical situation. France is accumulating both traditional problems of stratification and centralization and the new problems of the coming world of freedom and calculation. Still ill adapted to industrial society, France is already having to cope with the problems of post-industrial society. Paradoxically, it seems unable to admit that its problems stem from its poor capacity for collective action, and unwilling to remedy this. This complacency and reluctance to change are as marked in relations among social groups—in what we might call French society's systemic capacity—as in business and administrative matters.

I have already discussed the weaknesses of French organizations in some detail. Formal, rigid, incapable of developing efficient communication or participation, they waste resources and are far more interested in exploiting acquired advantages and the profits accruing from the status quo than in adjusting to new circumstances, grasping new opportunities, or innovating. As a result, they encourage neither the development of their members' freedom nor greater rationality in society as a whole.

And they have a poor capacity for growth. Everyone agrees that French businesses are too small. But we are inclined to believe that they are weak because they are small, when in fact it is the other way around: it is because they do not have the organizational capacity that they cannot grow; when one tries to make them grow too fast (as for example when they are forced into mergers), their real weaknesses develop as the fragmented bureaucratic apparatus becomes heavier. What is true for business is naturally true, *a fortiori,* for the government authorities, universities, hospitals, and indeed all French organizations.

But we should perhaps emphasize the "systemic" capacity of French society as a whole more strongly; that is to say, the possibility that French society (or its subsystems) could establish—among the various groups, organizations, classes, or sectors into which is divided—lines of communication, negotiation, conflict, and cooperation. These would permit a more exact appreciation of the facts in a given situation, the assumption of responsibility by the partners involved, and hence a generally more constructive process.

But systemic capacity is particularly weak in France. One gets the impression that every field—especially the most important of all integrative sectors, the political—is dominated by very cumbersome machinery, extremely fragile and at the same time highly resistant. Contacts are unreliable, bonds form barriers, communication is in the language of initiates, only false issues are raised, and the whole possesses an extraordinary inertial force. It is impossible to break the normal functioning of this machine; it discourages the best of good intentions and kills initiative. Also, once in motion, it is absolutely impossible to stop it, or even to correct or deflect its course.

Consider the example of the political parties, or the unions. These are confused, poorly integrated, and badly run,* but this

---

* The Communist Party is naturally an exception here, but its good management and overintegration only increase its rigidity, preventing it from engaging in any kind of fruitful or innovative exchange with its environment.

does not make them less rigid. On the contrary, given their impotence, they have to appeal to ideology in order to mobilize members, and sectarian fervor alone enables them to recruit and retain the bare minimum of responsible party or union workers. These well-meaning workers paradoxically then act as an exhausting constraint. As guardians of the ideology, the sole justification for their activities, they tend to paralyze the leadership, depriving it of any possibility of autonomous action and preventing it from maintaining contact with grass-roots supporters. They act as a screen; communication is impossible because of their use of jargon; insurmountable rigidity results. This rigidity is made still worse by the fragmentary nature of the organizations, incapable of acting alone yet incapable of communicating with one another. The system is at the same time fragile and sensitive to all kinds of blackmail. The gulf between the leaders and the led widens, decision-making becomes impossible, and the community is at the mercy of demagogic movements that may upset the mechanism completely for months or even years.

These mechanisms are not peculiar to unions or parties; they exist to a greater or lesser extent in all voluntary agencies and groups and, on a second level, in French society as a whole. Incapable of committing themselves or of making decisions, French leaders are continually expressing rigid public opinions that bear no relation to their private feelings. And the consequences of the social system's weak collective capacities becomes disastrous.

One essential feature of French society is that it is very hard to obtain knowledge of real social and human relationships within it—a direct result of the weakness of the society's collective capacity. With the possible exception of Italy, no other Western country reveals so great a distortion between official images (whether those of the country's government or of the opposition) and reality. In no other country is there such confusion in all the decision-making circuits. No other country is so reluctant to analyze its own mechanisms.

Curiously enough, it seems that French society knows itself

less well today than it did in 1900. When it was decided to construct the first Paris Métro, the decision-making process was truly open: serious studies were made (their accuracy and soundness have since been proved by the operational results), presented to the public, and discussed fully. In contrast, the construction of a new regional subway for Paris was decided on in an atmosphere of secret and complete confusion, and on the basis of widely false assumptions.

While the cities and the universities are the areas where this confusion is most blatant, we can see this same incapacity to face reality directly more or less everywhere. And not being able to face facts also means not being able to make decisions. To preserve his freedom of decision, the "decider" has himself protected by a series of screens; though he remains free, he is deprived of knowledge and cut off from the basic mechanisms operating in the areas where he intends to act. Despite the authoritarian façade, this bureaucratic approach only weakens him—since any argument can be acceptable in the absence of adequate factual knowledge. As a result, decision-making networks are continually snarled up by endless negotiations around rhetorical arguments that cannot be analyzed in the light of factual knowledge. Decisions are generally arrived at on the basis of false conflicts and in ignorance of the problems confronting those responsible for executing policy.

The phenomenon becomes pathological. Each time it looks as if progress is about to be made toward clarity, rigor, and freedom, one observes a kind of instinctive retreat back into the world of secrecy, privileges, and rents. The system depends on protections, which constitute the rules of the game. But the protections are never adequate and the system is always verging on panic, since the more one gives or concedes in this direction, the more the interested parties are frustrated, and the more they demand still further protection.

If this diagnosis is correct, the essential problem facing France concerns neither its growth nor its political regime nor socialism. It is quite simply the problem of the constitution and development of collective capacities that answer the needs of a complex society. This is not to deny the primary importance of growth or the aims of civilization. But, more and more, the development of a "systemic capacity" is an essential condition for sustained economic growth and for the democratization of society. All the vaunted ambitions of French reformers are nothing but rhetoric so long as they lack the courage to face squarely up to this problem.

But how can a society change? How can it move up from a system of mistrust, misunderstanding, and confusion to—not an ideal system, but one whose process is more open, more simple, more efficient? How can the members of society learn collectively?

Until now, it seems, human groups and societies transformed themselves in times of crisis. But crises rarely led to a true learning process. From this point of view, the dramatic thing about France in the years to come is that it is threatened by a series of breakdowns that are likely to have a regressive impact, while it might be able to carry out important transformations if they only could be turned into constructive crises inaugurating learning processes.

The true role of government in society, and that of all ruling groups in the organizations and institutions they control, would then be to provoke crises at the right time, in the right place, and in the right direction—as well as to make, ahead of and during these crises, the necessary institutional investments to ensure that the people and groups concerned will profit from them.

Education is, of course, the most important of all institutional investments. But not just any education. We tend to act as if only technical and rational training led to human advancement. But in fact the training upon which a society's capacity for development most depends is training aimed at improving a person's psychological capacity to withstand tension and conflict, to accept compromise, to overcome mistrust, to be more open to contact, and to assume greater freedom. The French are very poorly trained in this domain. Their personal psychological capacities are not in any way adapted to the problems they have to solve. Behind the façade of worker solidarity, just as behind the logic of castes, lies mutual distrust.

But education is only one aspect of the problem; it is ineffectual unless accompanied by parallel investments in new forms of organization and relationships. Any kind of experiment is an expensive undertaking, but without experiment one cannot accelerate the pace of development. The weakness of French organizational capacity is so great that an immense amount of experimenting will be needed to break out of its vicious circles of impotence and opposition. And, last, French society suffers from the mode of intellectual reasoning so closely associated with its anachronistic hierarchical and deductive tradition. Institutional investment must also be conceived in terms of intellectual institutions, since the way they function affects the development of new intellectual tools better adapted to our problems.

But the success of the collective learning process depends on the structures that condition the rules of play governing men in groups or organizations. And at this level the needed investments will have to be made as a function of crises.

The first of these constructive crises should be provoked around France's territorial structures. We have carried centralization about as far as it can go, to the point where we are now wholly blocked in a system we can no longer reform. Further reform merely encumbers it still further. A series of chains of dependency, from the summit to the base, keeps all levels of national, regional, and local power in tutelage, hence hierarchized. In the French political-administrative organization there is no intermediary power with sufficient authority to take initiatives and risks at its own level of information and representativity. All decisions are taken in the framework of the official—or semi-official—chains of command, the keystone being the central administrative bodies, in particular the Ministry of Finance. On top of this, all the technical experts to whom local authorities must turn are directly or indirectly connected with the civil-service hierarchies. This means that public collective initiatives are impossible without state authorization, state subsidies, and the state's technical experts.

This is not to say that officials of the Ministry of Finance or the *Service des Ponts et Chaussées* are incompetent; quite the reverse. Once one probes beyond the superficial defensive reflexes of local influential people, one finds that they usually have nothing but esteem and respect for the competence and devotion which the national officials are virtually alone in possessing. It is the government monopoly itself which constitutes the primary source of instability, forcing each of the actors to adopt a strategy based on dependence, on the presentation of claims and grievances, and on Malthusianism.

Only in rare cases do local or regional initiatives show evidence of a true sense of responsibility. Their main aim is to obtain state aid while avoiding risk. And, whatever their good intentions, national leaders never encounter anything but indifference, apathy, and hostility. This pattern is an extremely resilient one, since no one, at any level, is responsible for preserving it; it is held together essentially by the divergent demands of the various parties involved.

Then what institutional investments can French society be persuaded to make, through the government and public authorities, to conduct territorial experiments into more open systems of relations, relations whose modalities would favor innovation and responsibility? Whatever their cost, these investments would be far more profitable than the current scattering of subsidies chosen and controlled by the central authorities.

At the present time the weakest link in the chain—the regional link—has snapped. A first, very simple institutional investment at this level—the election of regional assemblies by universal suffrage—could be a point of departure for a constructive learning process. Of course this would provoke a crisis, but it could be directed and guided into constructive channels of development. The basic difficulty here is psychological. The day we can overcome this and ensure that the assemblies thus created will receive all the help they need in the early stages, we shall at last see the beginnings of an open process among the central authorities, in the external departments of public agencies, in prefectures and towns; then at last we can tackle all the problems that have beset us, particularly that of local finance.

But it is not enough to force the national administration to share its power with autonomous local and regional authorities. We must also break down the traditional mechanisms that block French society.

The civil service is in a state of crisis, but while its partial collapse makes it possible to innovate, this is not a solution in itself. We must agree to make investments in human training, and in the development of administrative institutions, without being afraid of the breakdowns these will inevitably entail. The only way to avoid explosions is to have the courage to provoke controlled crises.

What is the problem here?

The administrative system, as I have said, is less and less able to come to grips with reality, to communicate, to mobilize its resources, to adapt, or to innovate, because it is founded on the principle of protection, according to which decisions may suitably be made only by people separated—by buffer grades—from the problems to be dealt with, so that they do not directly confront the consequences of their actions. At the same time, the principle of protection also completely separates a person's career, which is governed by complex bureaucratic rules, from his real performance in his work.

It is easy enough to say what kind of reforms are needed. France must restructure the informal (or sometimes formal) hierarchy of administrative agencies that now vitiates the activities of at least two-thirds of the government (which is reduced to the role of a buffer grade acting on behalf of the Ministry of Finance). It must split up the immense monolith by splitting off all agencies whose function is to produce goods or services; they can be efficient only if their management is fully autonomous, and splitting them off will facilitate the functioning of the remainder. And it must develop a proper system of career-management, backed by permanent, effective, intellectually prestigious training institutions. These last should constantly re-evaluate tasks and performances, analyze the conditions in which they are carried out, and set up study units that could provide all government departments with the analytical capacities they now lack, organized in such a way as to stimulate creativity in these departments.

But these solutions are possible only if France will have the courage to make the necessary resources available—both men and money—so that the reforms are not merely legal ones or paper ones, but positive institutional investments.

It would be wholly inadequate merely to take power away from some in order to give to others, or to replace *a priori* by *a posteriori* controls. France must create bodies, systems of living relations capable of self-regulation, growth, and innovation, and thus gradually restore life to organizations now completely tied up in bureaucratic relationships. It must, finally, develop a much stronger systemic capacity among members of the administrative community, requiring everyone to express his personal view and to act responsibly.

Another knot in French administration—indeed in the entire system of government—is the continued existence of a certain number of closed *grands corps,* which traditionally appropriate not only all the high state positions but also most of the highest positions in nationalized industries and some of those in the biggest private corporations. The *grands corps* are going through a moral crisis, for their members no longer have the same profound faith in the virtues of the system which provides them with so many advantages. The younger generation criticizes the system's moral ideology, even if it remains consciously or unconsciously attached to its privileges. At all events, no one is now bold enough or crass enough to take control of an aristocratically based system with the right degree of authority.

The shake-up resulting from the crisis of May 1968 makes it possible to undertake thoroughgoing reforms, provided France has the will to generate and circumscribe the crisis around its central features. And indeed, it may be that no other breakdown, no institutional investment will have a greater effect than transforming and renovating the *grandes écoles*. The aim here should be neither to suppress them nor to drown them in a university complex capable only of very gradual reform, but to develop the considerable intellectual capital they already possess. Rather than continue supporting artificial advanced-technology industries at great expense, it would be far more beneficial to create, around the *Polytechnique* and the *Ecole Centrale*, two diversified and dynamic complexes comparable in influence to MIT or the Zurich *Polytechnicum*.

But the demise of the *grands corps* model should accompany the dismantling of the *grandes écoles* model. This appears quite feasible when one observes the uncertainty and unease prevailing in the higher reaches of the French administration. Its low level of morale could facilitate—no doubt via a problematical crisis—the radical transformation of the *grands corps* system. The state should be free to act like any ordinary employer; it must be able to recruit people from the best universities, thus offering a guarantee of real knowledge in specialties that are really needed, instead of committing itself to young people (and committing them along with it) whose principal quality is a sense of superiority in an anachronistic relationship.

The reform of the *grandes écoles* and the *grands corps* would of course have immediate repercussions on the management of private business as well. But in both private and public sectors another issue is moving toward the point of crisis: that of lower and middle management.

I have said that today's lower- and middle-management people derive their influence and importance from their positions as compulsory intermediaries in an organization governed by hierarchy and secrecy. Thus they are naturally opposed to any kind of transformation that is likely to lead to greater flexibility, clarity, or efficiency. Their reactions to the introduction of computers gave us an especially demonstrative example of this.

But competition leads ineluctably to greater efficiency. Many of these middle-level executives react to a threat to their traditional role by desperately clinging to an outmoded paternalist vision in which loyalty and fidelity are rewarded. Others join executive unions, based on the stratified concept of egalitarian defense of status, while others (less numerous) react more radically by claiming a share in management. But all these responses, conservative or radical, express a certain unease; they cannot really be said to offer any plausible solutions.

The problem these people are experiencing, in effect, is the one we have discussed in the abstract: how to learn to live in an environment based on freedom and calculation. The present behavior of French lower and middle management, asserting security and responsibility, loyalty and initiative, is pathologically escapist. Here again, institutional investment lies at the heart of the solution. France must train men who are capable of facing up to the tensions imposed by freedom, and we must develop structures and rules of play that make it profitable for individuals to take risks in a climate of cooperation.*

In the business world, scandalous speculation, unjustified profits, appalling inefficiency, and rank injustice are largely the result of the same systems of privilege whose mechanisms in the talent market we have analyzed.

The French economic system is still dominated in a great many fields by monopolies, agreements, restrictions, and forms of competition which in the final analysis are based on very conservative models of hierarchical stratification. At all levels, a whole series of laws, rules, administrative measures, and professional complicities restrict the opportunities for initiative, to the advantage of established people and institutions. Each sector of activity and every profession has more or less

---

* The problem is complicated by the fact that the management-executive community is heavily favored in terms of income. If certain exceptional performances are less well recognized and remunerated than they would be in the United States, for example, average performances are treated most advantageously in comparison to most white-collar or blue-collar workers'. It might then be thought that direct material interest is at stake in this mode of government. But one can hope that accelerated expansion, which could be made possible by improving the business management system, would lead to more equitable income distribution, without managers' and executives' necessarily being victimized.

succeeded in developing its own closed-shop model. One must belong to the club if one wishes to live and prosper, but admission to the club is closed to newcomers.

The state plays a vital role in preserving these caste privileges in the business world—first on account of the links between the government and business castes at the top, but above all because state aid is managed so that it almost exclusively benefits vested economic interests. It thus helps to preserve these interests and operates most of the time to the detriment of really new initiatives.*

The effects of this system are prejudicial to relations among corporations themselves, but they also affect a person's capacity for initiative and his chances of success. The fact that an imaginative engineer can practically never leave an employer who deprives him of the opportunity to set up a rival concern has a deadening effect. Convinced in advance that the banks, dominated by traditional solidarities, will reject his application for credit, that it is useless to hope for state aid since this is handed out by the "club," the engineer will fritter his talents away in fruitless intrigues.

So it is crucial that we undertake a thoroughgoing reform of the existing competitive system and the mechanisms of innovation, if we are to inject greater dynamism into the French economy and encourage greater creativity among French executives, engineers, and managers. Is this going to be possible? It may be that the illness is not yet visible enough (except in a number of sectors, such as real estate). But people are now becoming increasingly aware of the incredible economic and social rigidities crippling French society. We should exploit the energies of all those who instinctively favor genuine reform of the system, instead of diverting and wasting them in ideological games.

French society oscillates between stability, which confines

---

* Of course it frequently happens that dynamic government administrators enthusiastically back some new discovery, process, or innovative business. But these are only exceptions that prove the usual rule.

each of the "socio-professional categories" or "driving forces" to immobility—playing its role by rote and without conviction —and, on the other hand, revolutionary panic. The system is sick, its impoverishment has become a matter of great concern, and it no longer serves a society whose needs are far more numerous and in which the variables to be taken into account are more complex than ever before. We shall cure it when the entire circuit—citizens, party workers, and leaders—is revitalized. This requires the elimination of ideological gimmicks and of the permanent conflict over which problems belong at what level and which are directly related to the "great cause." Political decentralization is one condition of change, but another important one is analysis and criticism of the systems in which the actors are involved—systems which the leaders for the most part either are unaware of or else leave out of account.

It is true that crises do threaten the stability of the whole of French society in sectors where the acceleration of change has made the existing system anachronistic; this has been true in agriculture, among small shopkeepers, and in a few declining industries. The short-term response to these crises has been the temporary palliative of subsidies or the imposition of restrictive and protective rules. But the real issue lies in the innovative capacity of the system itself: agriculture's modern capacities have never really been utilized, and they have in fact been discouraged by the total ignorance that prevails about how in fact the human system which constitutes French agriculture is regulated, and how it might be changed. In the case of the small tradesmen, no effort has ever been made to discover how the transformations now in progress are perceived by them. We condemn on principle, without seeking to understand.

It is not surprising, therefore, that the cycle of change imposed on society involves, in chronological order: (1) a brilliant, rigorous technocratic attack on a specific problem, which is nonetheless blind and clumsy; (2) a stubborn and equally blind defense, mobilizing opinion to the extremes of sentimentality; (3) shameless, successful blackmail, particularly effective in that it enjoys public support; (4) blind negotiation, whose problematic outcome is of no real use even to those concerned.

In order to transform this, systems of relationships must occur in which the various antagonists become aware of systemic necessities, and in which they are encouraged to accept the risks entailed in an evolutionary process that is likely to benefit them. Instead of blaming mean-minded, reactionary opponents, it is more useful to try to understand the system of economic and human relations in which problems such as those of parasitic small shopkeepers, say, or marginal agricultural holdings or paternalistic family businesses could crystallize, how the systems that made them possible evolved, and how the people concerned can perceive the benefits that will accrue to them if they abandon their defensive strategies.

Toward a Strategy of Change

Throughout this brief examination of the problems that French society is going to have to deal with, and the crises that ought to be provoked if the French are to succeed, I have constantly emphasized the one essential, inescapable priority of institutional investment. I want to come back to this one last time, because the strategy of change I want to propose effectively depends on it.

Every discussion concerning objectives and choices—dealing with industrial policy, urban development, planning, or social progress—always turns on the results we want to achieve, that is to say, on our definition of the hoped-for final form of the society, sector, or problem under consideration. If, for example, we want to make the university more democratic, or stabilize social-security expenditures, or make the machine-tool industry more competitive, we must organize the available means as a function of these objectives. The state, as the main contractor, assumes responsibility for executing the program. It desperately tries to control this program, unaware that its methods of encouragement, subsidy, and control generally work against the goals it is pursuing.

Modern problems of change cannot usefully be dealt with in this manner. If it really is true that France's problems are so acute because its organizational and systemic capacity is so feeble, then clearly the most fundamental problem the country has is to improve its collective capacities. What we call institutional investment is the painful, politically troublesome, costly effort involved in fostering the gradual development of systems of relations and negotiation, bodies of rules and customs, and more complex, open, comprehensive, and efficient regulatory models.

Institutional investment works directly when the state plays a central role; it may work very indirectly in an economic sphere only marginally linked to the public authorities or when it concerns the internal affairs of a private organization. But in all cases the state's role in society is now crucially important both in financial and regulatory affairs, and in the social and psychological spheres.

How should we go about making these institutional investments? Can we really reverse priorities so that they *can* be made? In my opinion, the problem is not one of financial resources or even political priorities; it is primarily a problem of intellectual conversion.

Naturally, human and financial resources are limited, and any government's political ability to act is minimal. But governmental impotence stems far more from the fact that its resources and capacities are already committed elsewhere, tied up in maintaining supporting activities whose results are useless so long as the organizational or systemic capacities remain weak. We can escape from this powerlessness by learning to concentrate the collectivity's resources at key points in the systems now caught in these deplorable vicious circles. This is far preferable to accepting responsibility for the consequences of present malfunctions, since this only helps to perpetuate them.

In order to achieve this, we should encourage three principal intellectual approaches in all activities concerning the management of society. First, priority should be given to the development of a capacity for serious analysis. Political, administrative, and even economic leaders are stifling beneath the weight of countless brilliant syntheses, but they are not in possession of the kind of analytical ability needed to make decisions concerning the future. No program or administrative action should be launched before a proper diagnosis has been made of the complex system within which it will operate. As long as we lack knowledge of the system's knots of power and modes of regulation, even the most attractive undertakings will result in wastage. (The current vogue for business and administrative consultancies is a bogus response to this need; studies are being carried out to justify existing practices, not in order to understand them.) Investment in analytical capability is now more urgent than any form of economic investment, however modernistic.

The second approach should be concerned with understanding the process of change itself and the appropriate types of behavior for controlling it. No serious change can avoid the painful reversal of deeply rooted habits. (A truly comprehensive analysis of practices shows that they are frequently rational, even beneficial, in their own terms.) And this kind of reversal almost always occurs with an accompanying crisis. We are both fascinated by and dreadfully afraid of these crises. We need to learn how to provoke them and to guide them along the right channels.

The third approach concerns our attitude toward institutions. Now we refuse to be bothered with them. Only the individual and the law (or the government, or the administration, or the revolution) count. But it is impossible to carry out a program or attain an objective unless there is some formal or informal institution to manage the results. We seem prepared to legislate for education or health, but no one wants to learn about the mechanisms involved in founding, managing, developing, or inspiring a social agency as complex as a university or a hospital. Yet a society's capacity for action, its ability to reveal its own problems, to discover solutions to them and to put these solutions into effect, and its aptitude for innovation, all depend essentially upon its institutional resources. Formal or informal, institutions are the instruments of human cooperation. There can be no more exalted task than to be concerned in their development. Imagination is not enough here. We must summon up other virtues whose intellectual qualities have long been forgotten, of which the most important are patience and courage.